HAUNTINGS & HEALINGS

And other such wonders from the paranormal experiences of psychic medium and healer

Helen Bevan

AuthorHouse™
1663 Liberty Drive
Bloomington, IN 47403
www.authorhouse.com
Phone: 1-800-839-8640

© 2011 All Rights Reserved. Helen Bevan.

No part of this book may be reproduced, stored in a retrieval system,
or transmitted by any means without the written permission of the author.

First published by AuthorHouse 10/4/2011

ISBN: 978-1-4567-9843-7 (sc)

Printed in the United States of America

This book is printed on acid-free paper.

Because of the dynamic nature of the Internet, any web addresses or links contained in this book may have changed since publication and may no longer be valid. The views expressed in this work are solely those of the author and do not necessarily reflect the views of the publisher, and the publisher hereby disclaims any responsibility for them.

To my young friend, Rachael, who first inspired me to write this book when she said, aged 8, that when I wrote a book she would keep it by her bed.

Photos taken by, or belong to, either Helen or Keith unless otherwise stated.

The diamond at the beginning of Chapter 17 is from Wikipedia:-
- Beschreibung: Diamanten
- Info: Fotografiert von Mario Sarto 04. Februar 2004
- Lizenz: GNU Free Documentation License

PART ONE

		Page
1	My early upbringing	5
2	Keith enters my life	9
3	Twinkle & Misty	12
4	Our firstborn	15
5	Our involvement with Spiritualism	19

PART TWO

6	Residual Energies	28
7	Helping souls cross over	31
8	Hallowe'en Ghostwatch	40
9	Fighting the good fight	46
10	Animal Tales	48
11	Clairvoyance	54
12	Spirit guidance	58
13	Mysterious ways	65
14	Healing	70
15	Sacred spaces	81
16	Past lives	84

PART THREE

17	Your Higher Self	90
18	Energies and Dimensions	92
19	Opening Sacred Spaces	95
20	Closing Down	97
21	Poems	99
22	Affirmations	102

PART ONE

My early life; and my discovery of things paranormal.

"There are no unnatural or supernatural phenomena, only very large gaps in our knowledge of what is natural".

Edgar Mitchell
Astronaut

My Early Upbringing

Me in 1953

I had my first psychic experience when I was about eight years old. I was, for the very first time, trusted to be in the house on my own. It was a 1930s semi-detached with a large garden – big enough, if you wanted, to put a lawn tennis court in. My parents had taken my brother somewhere - maybe to the dentist or to buy him some shoes - and I felt proud to have been allowed to stay on my own. I wanted to do something to show them how responsible I was. So when they were due back I went to the kitchen and stood, in this empty house, wondering what to do – when I heard a voice say "Well, put the kettle on then!"

I was thrilled – I thought God had spoken to me, but at the same time I was disappointed that the only time He had spoken to me He had said something so mundane! I now realise that it was more likely to have been my maternal Grandmother who had passed away when I was six, but I put the kettle on anyway and earned my Brownie points.

Where I grew up

I was born not long after the Second World War, the youngest of three children. My sister had been born before the war and was therefore much older than me (or so it seemed at the time) but my brother was only three years older.

We were brought up in the way typical for the period by decent, hardworking, caring parents. We had no particular religion, except just generally Christian, but we were encouraged to go to the local non-denominational Mission.

Our upbringing was nothing out of the ordinary, and I had no knowledge, let alone experience, of things psychic. It was not until much later that I learnt my maternal Grandmother had held séances in her home (to which my father had gone whilst courting my mother), used a crystal ball and could read tea leaves, as could her eldest daughter, whose own son, my cousin, became a healer.

I also learnt much later, that my maternal Grandmother's own mother had refused to emigrate to America with her husband in the 1880s because she had been told by a clairvoyant "not to cross the water". If she had then this story could have been very different! As, indeed, it would also have been had my father known that he had been offered a teaching post in Glasgow, whilst I was still at school. Too late, Dad discovered that the letter offering him the job had been pushed under the door and had gone completely out of sight under the lino!

The next psychic experience I remember was when I was about twelve. I had agreed to meet a friend outside Bristol University one Saturday. I got there far too early so decided to while away the time by going around the Red Lodge, a fine old building constructed in the late 1580s. The only other person there was the curator, who was downstairs.

I sauntered around the rooms trying to imagine what life would have been like when the house was lived in – father standing with his back to the living room fireplace, mother sewing in the armchair, young children playing on the floor whilst older ones sat reading in the window alcove...

Then I moved onto the next room – a small, dark bedroom with a four-poster bed and panelling all in dark wood – I didn't like it so I moved to the doorway to the next room (the doors had been removed). The next room was sparsely furnished and quite light and yet I felt petrified. Not being one to give in to my fears, I took a deep breath and dashed through the room. Whereupon the feeling of fear vanished, leaving me only with a pounding heart! I told my friend and then forgot about it - that is until it happened again about two years later! It took me several days to remember the previous incident, but when I did I determined to go back and see if it would happen again.

This time, of course, I was not able to relax quite so much even though I tried to recreate the same feelings as I'd had before. Nonetheless, when I came to that doorway I still felt the fear even though it was less strong. This time I was able to stand in the room and look at a picture on the wall. I have no idea what the picture was like, as I felt as though someone was approaching me from behind with a dagger raised for my back. I fled.

Me in 1961

In 1963 I took eight GCE 'O' levels at Rose Green High School for Girls, in Whitehall. I wasn't sure what I wanted to do after that so I planned to attend several career lectures at Bristol University the winter before the exams. But Fate intervened. The weather that year was so atrocious that I was only able to attend one of the lectures - the one on Librarianship.

At that time you could enter Library School with either two 'A' levels or the First Professional Exam (plus appropriate 'O' levels of course). I had decided that was definitely what I wanted to do, so I reasoned that I might as well be getting some practical experience, and be getting paid for it, as taking the 'A' levels. Accordingly I took a job with Bristol Public Libraries. In those days of full employment it didn't even cross your mind that you might not be able to get the job you wanted.

The first four months I worked at Fishponds Library, and then transferred to St. George Library in the January, which was much nearer to my home. This was not the magnificent old Victorian Library that I had used as a child, but the new, modern library that had only been opened the previous November. We started work at 9 o'clock in the morning, but didn't open to the public until half-past. The first job for everyone in the mornings at all the libraries was to go around straightening the shelves - that is putting them tidy and in order. I was a happy soul and used to sing or hum to myself as we straightened the shelves.

This particular week started as usual except that I felt a bit subdued and didn't feel like singing. The following day I felt worse, and the day after, until by Thursday I was thinking 'what's the point of going on? I might as well end it all.' Various methods of doing so went through my mind, until I decided that if I was going to I would do it with aspirins. Another part of me was saying 'what are you doing? What's wrong with you? O.K. so you haven't got a boyfriend, but that's never worried you before, so what's the problem?' So I just hung in there thinking it must be one of those phases Mum kept saying I was going through.

On the Saturday I woke up feeling fine – back to normal. At that time my sister was married and living not too far away, so I determined to go and see her and tell her about these strange feelings I'd been having all week. But when I got there she had a tale to tell!

The previous Sunday she had been sorting out her husbands' clothes to send to the cleaners when she came across a letter in his pocket from another woman. She didn't say anything to him as she was so stunned and needed time to think. It had been preying on her mind all week, making her more and more depressed. By the Friday she had decided to leave him, so she walked out and wandered the streets for a while, until she realised that she had nowhere to go (having badly fallen out with our parents over this same man). She went back to the lower part of the house, poured a glass of port and fetched a bottle of aspirins. As she was about to take the first of the aspirins her husband walked in, realised what she was doing and smashed the lot out of her hands. They talked about the whole thing and kissed and made up.

I had obviously been picking up some of this psychically somehow, and if I hadn't been such a strong character I might have succumbed to these feelings and no-one would have known why. I now believe that it was only because I was so strong that this was allowed to happen, and that somehow it helped my sister to get through it.

Later, when I was working in the Children's Library at the Bristol Central Library, I experienced another strange phenomenon. I worked there for four months from October 1965. We didn't have a phone of our own, so shared the one at the main desk. I found that when I listened to it ringing I could tell whether it was for us or not, and if it was I would be waiting to be beckoned over. The only times I was wrong was when it was for both of us and they dealt with the caller first.

In early January 1966 the Deputy City Librarian sent for me. He told me he especially wanted me to go to St Phillips Branch Library as sub to a newly appointed Branch Librarian.

This was Bristol's first Branch - big, draughty and with a very old-fashioned lay-out. Consequently it was generally considered a place that one would be sent to as a kind of punishment, which is why the Deputy City Librarian had taken the unusual step of sending for me, as he wanted to make sure that I knew I had been specially chosen to help change this image. He said he wanted someone "decent, hard-working, and with courage". The following day the new Branch Librarian told me she had ordered two nylon overalls for us! My diary entry for Jan 24th – my first day there – states, "it really is filthy "

In the May, my previous boss from the Children's' Library, who was also interested in the paranormal, took me to see a psychometrist – someone who can hold objects and get from them information about their owners.

We joined a roomful of people in this old Victorian house, and each person put an object on a tray at the front. I put my watch.

At the appointed time a gentleman entered the room and began to give a reading from each object. From my watch he said that he could hear wedding bells for me. This did not impress me as I had only recently met Keith, didn't intend to get serious as I would soon be off to London for two years to study Librarianship, and was building up to breaking it off with him - but it turned out that he was right.

Keith Enters My Life

Keith & me on our wedding day

I first met Keith in March 1966 when we both went to the Central Hall in Bristol, with different Young Socialist groups, to a pre-election meeting featuring Harold Wilson. Before the meeting started, Keith had approached the people I was with, whom he knew, asking to be introduced to this new girl – I remember thinking that he smelled of potatoes (he had come straight from working in a warehouse where he had been handling sacks of various foods, but sacks to me meant potatoes). Afterwards both groups went for a drink together in The Wheatsheaf, from where I remember Keith's lovely blue eyes. Talk turned to a forthcoming party and when I said I could probably get my brother to borrow our Dad's car everyone was trying to persuade me to go (bear in mind that very few young people had cars in those days, or even access to them – Keith's parents never had a car, and mine had only acquired one a few years previously).

The day of the party came, and the boy I had been interested in had not gone. The others that I had also been interested in had, one by one, had too much to drink. After someone had mixed my drinks and I had poured it down the kitchen sink, I stood looking around considering my options. At that point Keith, who I knew had not been drinking as he was a co-driver with a friend, plonked himself down in an armchair and opened his arms to me – the boldest move I think he has ever made! I hesitated, but thought 'why not? I don't have anything else in mind', so I went and sat on his lap!

He looked so young that, despite the fact that he was four years older than me, I was accused of 'baby-snatching'! (I was almost 18 and he was coming up for 22).

Some considerable time later, whilst in a car with him and his brother, I was telling them of the time I had canoed 55 miles down the River Wye with my brother in a double canoe he had built, when Keith's brother interrupted to say that he had talked a year or two before to a girl that had done that – then he looked at me, did a double take, and said 'it was you, wasn't it?' It was indeed.

At that time I had been going out with someone else and had gone to a show at the old Pro-Cathedral that my boyfriend was compèring. I had been seated by a friend of his, but when she had to leave to help with the teas in the interval she had brought someone over to sit with me. That someone turned out to be Keith's brother, and if I hadn't told him such a unique and memorable tale we would never have remembered that we had met before! As well as that, when my boyfriend the compère had invited two people to join him on stage his friend who was sitting with me and a man from elsewhere in the hall had gone up – that man had been Keith! They all knew each other! But Keith was with another girl at that time, so the time was not right for us to meet.

He tells me that one night, after he had broken up with that other girl, he was laying in bed thinking 'I wonder what the girl I'll marry will be like?' It popped into his head that she would wear glasses and would go to college. He thought, glasses, fair enough, he had gone out with girls who had worn glasses, but a college girl? No way – him go out with a college girl? Yet six months after we started going out together I went to college (and I've worn glasses since I was 11).

The only other paranormal experience he'd had was when he was a schoolboy. He would pick up other peoples' conditions – e.g. if someone had a limp he would be unable to stop himself from limping too. If anyone had seen him they would have thought he was taking the mickey! I have recently discovered that this is a recognized condition that goes by the name of echopraxia. Now, when he does healing or gives messages he often does the same, but knows this is being clairsentient, and a valuable aid to helping them.

A little later, whilst working in the warehouse, he had distinctly heard someone call 'Keith' – but when he looked there was no-one there – an early example of clairaudience.

Much later Keith told me that about a fortnight after meeting me he had told his father that I was the girl he was going to marry – long before he ventured to suggest it to me. Mind you, we nearly didn't make it!

After we had been going out for 2½ months I began to feel that there was no future in this relationship, and was thinking of ending it. Trouble was, I didn't want to hurt Keith, as he'd been so nice to me, and had been hurt before. However, six weeks later I had decided that I couldn't allow it to carry on like this, so tonight was the night, but when I got to Keith's house he presented me with a box of chocolates – just because I had been niggly for a few weeks! How could I finish with him then?

When we were courting we went to various churches, trying to find one we could attend regularly and that we both felt comfortable with. Some were better than others, being more friendly, but none of them felt right, because we could not believe all the things they believed. So in the end we gave up and decided we must be atheists. However, we couldn't quite manage that, as we felt there had to be some power such as people call God. So we became agnostics – willing to believe if proof could be given, or at least strong evidence. Little did we realise what was to follow!

From September 1966 to July 1968 I attended Ealing Technical College doing Library Studies. The first term I stayed with two other girls in a bed-sit where we were allowed no visitors except girls on Sundays, and where we were told that 4d (about 2p in today's money) would get us 4" (about 10cms) of water in the bath "which was enough for anybody"! The landlady had also complained about the heavy footsteps across our room, when it was only one of us walking normally, and in slippers at that! Not surprisingly we soon began looking around for somewhere else.

We found a lovely flat at the top of a house owned by an Iranian (or Iraqi, I can't remember which now) and occupied by his son and daughter who also went to college. The daughter was very restricted and was not allowed to go anywhere but college, even having to ask her brother first if she wanted to buy something in a shop on the way home. However, they did not care what we did. The flat was for four, so another girl joined us. She was engaged and her fiancé used to come to stay at the weekends, as did Keith. Unfortunately at the end of the first academic year the Middle East war flared up again, they were both called back home, and the place sold, so we had to find somewhere else for the last year.

The place we found was the upstairs of a semi-detached house near Hangar Lane, all except one room which was the bedroom of one of the men who lived there. There were two men and one woman who spoke little, but we understood them to be unrelated Polish survivors of the concentration camp at Dachau. The main one we spoke to was an accountant. This time we were allowed visitors, but not after 10p.m.

At first Keith had hired a vehicle every so often to come up to see me at weekends, staying in a B&B, but that proved expensive and not often enough. So then, after finishing work every Friday, he would get onto the Bath Road and hitch-hike (remember this was before the days of the motorways – the M4 was still being built while I was at college), and stay in our top floor flat.

By the second year, Keith and I were engaged and he was visiting every weekend. He again stayed in bed and breakfast accommodation nearby, but it was often after 10pm when he arrived. We found that most times his lifts would drop him off at the Chiswick flyover from where it was a 45 minute walk. The quickest he did the journey was two and a half hours in a Triumph Vitesse, the longest was about eight hours, the average being three to four hours. I found that I could somehow know when he was dropped off and if that meant he would arrive after 10pm I would prepare some food and drink, put it in a duffle bag, and we would catch a train somewhere and walk and talk, returning early in the morning. The only time I was caught out was when he was dropped off much nearer, but the timing would have been right otherwise.

When Keith and I got married in August 1968 we set up house in a flat above a hardware shop, which was mostly already furnished. Our bedroom had thin curtains and a street lamp outside, so was never really dark. The bed was under the window facing the door. Behind the door was an old wardrobe with our blankets just showing above the façade at the top. At that time Keith was driving lorries and was often away overnight.

On one such night I was woken suddenly from my sleep by I know not what. I opened my eyes and saw the wardrobe in front of me, but instead of our blankets there were cardboard boxes on top (one looking as if it might fall off) and a modern-looking powder-blue travelling bag, with lots of pockets and straps. Several thoughts went through my mind in rapid succession – where did they come from? Was the box going to fall off? And how come I could see the colour of the bag when the rest of the room was only shapes and shadows? As I stared at them they slowly faded away – and there were our blankets.

About a fortnight later Keith was again away overnight. This time I was wide awake – I just could not seem to get to sleep! Knowing I would be unfit for work in the morning if I didn't, I determinedly shut my eyes but still could not sleep. Suddenly, for no reason, my eyes flew open and there, just inside the bedroom door, behind the chest of drawers, was a young woman! She was dressed in a bright red wet-look hat, with blonde curls peeping out, and a short, beige, wet-look coat. She appeared to be looking at me and yet not – as if she was not really seeing what was before her. I assumed she was a burglar and my mind raced – how had she got in? Everything was locked, and I had not heard any noise! How could I defend myself if she attacked me? What funny clothes for a burglar to be wearing – and anyway how could I see the colours? All this time – only a few seconds – I was staring at her, then she began to rise up into the air in an arc! I couldn't believe what I was seeing! I screwed my eyes up for a second and when I opened them again she had gone!

Obviously not a burglar, but what? I lay there with my heart pounding, but in the morning I checked all the windows and the door. All was as it should be.

At that time I was working in the Bristol Central Lending Library, so had loads of different books passing through my hands. I came across one called 'Forty Years a Medium', by Ursula Roberts, which I found fascinating. It kept referring to a book called 'This is Spiritualism', by Maurice Barbanell, so I read that one afterwards in my lunch breaks. It was as if this man had all the pieces of my jigsaw (my thus far unexplained paranormal experiences), plus some, and had made them into this picture called 'Spiritualism'! I realised that I had to share this with Keith or else he would end up married to a stranger, it was changing me that much! So each evening I would go home and tell Keith all about it – until one day he told me to bring the book home and he would read it. (He is not a reader – he has only read a handful of books in his whole adult life). At that time Maurice Barbanell was the editor of 'Psychic News', a weekly newspaper, and his book frequently referred to happenings in Spiritualist churches.

I was quite happy just to know that all my experiences and thoughts added up to something recognisable, but Keith wanted more - he wanted to go to one of the churches.

Working in the library it was easy to find out where there were some. In Kelly's Directory for Bristol it listed six. We decided to try all six, starting with the one at Bedminster. However when we looked for it one Sunday evening we couldn't find it – we discovered later it had moved a few years earlier. We also discovered later that there were not six but at least ten - and so started our long association with Spiritualism, which I will tell you about later.

Twinkle & Misty

Some months before we were married, while Keith was living alone in the flat above the hardware shop, we had adopted two kittens from the litter of his sister's cat. We had intended to get the black and white one, but she was very nervous and wouldn't come near us, yet her sister, a tabby, curled up on Keith's lap - so we took both of them home on the bus with us, Keith carrying the black and white one, and me the tabby one. We named them Twinkle and Misty respectively.

I'm very glad we got two as they were delightful to watch together and were company for each other when we were out at work.

It took Twinkle a fortnight before she would allow us to approach her, but thereafter she was a lovely companion to us but extremely wary of strangers. Misty, on the other hand, was a very friendly cat and loved to be made a fuss of by any passing stranger. She was also a very sympathetic cat – anytime I was feeling low, sitting and crying, she would come and put her paws on me, looking up at me with such a look of concern that it never failed to put a smile on my face, albeit a watery one. I used to throw a small holey red plastic ball up the stairs to bounce against the wall and come back down. She would race up after it, and then back down again, time and time again, giving her maximum exercise for my minimum effort.

They were nearly four years old when I was first pregnant. It was a very hot summer and I was heavily pregnant, due in just four days, when Misty disappeared. I searched all over the village, calling her name and looking for her collar with her name tag on.

Our son was born on the day he was due, and I spent ten days in the maternity home, as was usual then. On the day before I was due home Keith told me he had felt Misty around him, so we knew she was dead. I learnt later that many local cats had been disappearing around that time, and she was so friendly she would not have been difficult to steal. I sobbed my heart out that night, much to the Matrons' displeasure who thought Keith should not have told me until I had gone home. I guess it upset her routine.

At least it meant that Misty had not suffered for more than a fortnight. Some time after I got home, I was lying curled up in bed when I felt her settle down in the crook of my knees – where she always settled, and it was comforting to know she was still with us.

I later wrote this poem:-

A Tribute to Misty

Misty – as impenetrable as her name,
Her thoughts veiled over by candid eyes,
Staring unblinkingly from her owlish face.

Misty – light and agile, quick and playful,
Darting up and down and in and out;
Keen and quiet, gentle and graceful.

Misty – curled up in warm affection,
Ecstatically purring sweet endearments,
Softly, contentedly, snuggling close.

Misty – stalking noiselessly through the grass,
Tensely crouching, swiftly springing;
Another victim proudly carried home.

Misty – an enigma among cats:
Loving, but free; independent, yet sympathetic.
Remembered and symbolised by her small, red, ball.

Twinkle was very wary of the new baby, and would only cautiously approach him.

For the first three months of his life Beric slept in his carrycot at the foot of our bed, and in the morning I would lift it onto my stomach, carry it down the stairs, along the hall, and put it in a stand in the diner. I got quite fast at it.

One morning I had carried it as far as the hall and was halfway along it when the thought flashed through my mind – 'I haven't seen the cat this morning!' I stopped dead with one foot in mid-motion and looked underneath the carrycot – there was Twinkle happily cleaning herself, with the tip of my foot only an inch away. One more second and I would have kicked her square on her back and sent her flying! Probably breaking her back and maybe dropping the baby and injuring us all. Thank you spirit friends!

Twinkle lived until she was 14 years old and going deaf – she was run over by what she probably thought was a parked car, but it was waiting to turn out of a side road opposite our house. The lady driver offered me a lift with the cat to the vet. I sat in the back with Twinkle on my lap. She showed no physical sign of injury, but had mewed pitifully and with such pain in her eyes. I suddenly became aware of her standing alongside me, so I knew that she had died. But at least, at the end, she was with someone she loved, and who loved her.

Thoughts of Twinkle

O Beautiful pussy warm by my side,
What thoughts do those furry brows hide?
Green eyes! – Narrow slits of contentment;
Do you know the sharp pang of resentment?

Safe in the knowledge of love freely given,
By no great ambition are you driven,
Happy just feeding and sleeping and loving –
With such strength and grace, moving.

O Beautiful black and white pussycat
Purring so softly, curled up on my lap,
Can you tell me the secret of your life so serene?
Can you show me the way to your pastures green?

Our Firstborn

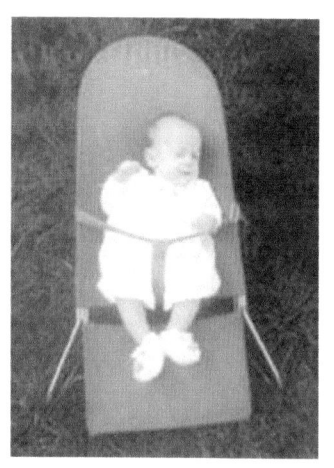

Beric, aged 3 months

Anyone who has had a new baby will know that you sleep very lightly in case they need you in the night. Beric, our first-born, was born in July 1972. One night during the first three months, when Keith was at work, I woke to see a tall upright figure with his arms stretched out in front of him, palms up, walking slowly through the part-open door, and indeed, through the door-frame he was so tall. My immediate reaction was that he had come to take my baby away, at which he disappeared and too late did I realise that he had in fact come with a gift for the baby. I got the impression that he was a Native American. On feeling my fear he had simply vanished. I only hope that I did not deprive Beric of his gift.

Breastfeeding my baby one night I remembered what I had heard an experienced midwife was reported to have said – that when a baby was very young she could look at it and 'see' what he/she would become in adult life, whether a doctor, teacher or whatever. I thought I'd try this, so looked at Beric, suckling contentedly, but instead of the future I tried to go back to a past life. I 'saw' that he had been a gladiator in Roman times!

One morning, when Beric was about 16 months old, he was in his highchair in the kitchen/diner being fed his breakfast. I had my back to the kitchen as I tried to get him to eat. I could hear a cat lapping milk or water from the bowls behind me, but could not understand why Beric would not eat his food and was so intently watching our cat.

Eventually I gave up trying to get him to accept his food and turned around to say hello to Twinkle – but she was not there! I found she was still on the bed where I had left her. It must have been Misty! No wonder Beric was so interested – he would not have seen a tabby cat around the house before – if you remember, she disappeared four days before he was born.

Another time, when I had given him his bath, he kept pointing around the bathroom, desperately trying to get me to see "silver balls" which were obviously moving around at about his head height and above. To quieten him I had to say that I saw them too, though in truth I could not.

Almost every night for the first 18 months Beric cried and cried. We took it in turns to go and see if he was too hot or too cold, wet, hungry… Nothing seemed to make any difference, so eventually we just let him cry himself to sleep – night after night.

Then on his second Christmas, by which time he was getting about a bit, we put up the usual six-foot Christmas tree with decorations – and put a wooden playpen in the room to put him in, to keep him away from it.

Every time we put him in it he would create merry hell! Eventually we put the Christmas tree in it instead, and solved the problem that way.

It made us realise that it was the same with his cot-bed. We took the wooden bars away and he was fine after that! Much later we were told that in a past life he had been a Native American half-caste called Injun Joe, so we thought he had probably suffered behind bars in that life.

Beric, 3, with Xmas tree in playpen

He couldn't have been much older than this when spirit intervened on his behalf. When I was working in the kitchen we had a baby gate across the kitchen door, as well as one at the bottom of the stairs. Beric had the run of the front room and the hallway.

I didn't realise it at the time but I was suffering from post-natal depression. It didn't feel like depression to me – I was frequently losing my temper, something I had never done before. Oh, I had got cross, yes – but never had I really lost my temper. And now I was doing it several times a day! When this happened when I was bathing Beric, as it often did, I had learnt to let my feelings out by banging the side of the bath or the door, or hitting myself - anything to avoid hitting my baby, as I had found that even what I had thought was a gentle tap had left the pink imprint of my hand on his skin. I got no help with this because when the nurses asked if Beric was a good baby I had to say yes, because I could not conceive of any baby being bad. If they had asked a different question they would have got the answer they should have – I was finding it far from easy!

On this particular occasion I was working at the sink in a not very good mood which was getting worse by the minute as Beric stood by the gate pestering me with questions.
Eventually I snapped and swung round with my hand raised in the air ready to hit him – but as I turned it was if a cloak of anger had been instantaneously lifted from me and I was left standing there feeling surprised, ashamed, foolish, relieved - and grateful.

I had hidden my feelings from everyone except Keith as I felt ashamed of them. I struggled to control them, and pretended to everyone else, including my mother, that everything was fine. Without Keith's help and support, and the help from spirit, I don't know how I would have got through those difficult years. I often used to put Beric safely into his cot, close the intervening doors, and throw myself onto the settee in the front room in floods of tears.
When Keith came home from work and found me in a foul mood he would often put on a relaxing tape which, despite myself, would calm me down. It was only when I was pregnant a second time, and confided to my doctor my fears of going through that again, that I learnt that it was post-natal depression. He gave me Valium to get me through from then on, which I took only half a tablet at a time, now and then, as I found any more and I couldn't function properly.
Even then I would sometimes be waiting for Keith to come home so that I could escape and go for a long walk on my own.
I discovered that I don't like anyone or any living thing being totally dependent on me, including animals and plants!

When Beric was about 2½ he tried to tell me, in his baby talk, that he had seen two men looking at his baby sister in her carrycot. I saw no-one when I went in to look and assumed he was pretending whilst playing with his toys. However, over three years later, our spirit friend, Shaun O'Rafferty, told us that he had been one of the three men.

My relationship with my son was a battle of wills and one day whilst pondering why this should be, my past life memory opened and showed me a time when we were both alive in the days of Ancient Rome. As I mentioned before my son was at that time a gladiator. I saw myself as a woman accompanying the most important man of the town to the games. I watched as my son (now) fought a very good fight with another gladiator, but eventually lost. As was the custom then, the victor looked towards the main man to see if he gave the thumbs up or down, indicating life or death. It had been such a well-fought match that the decision was obvious – the thumbs up, so the man indicated that I should make the decision. As a woman I did not have much power at all in my life, and if I had given the thumbs up I would not have been exercising any power, merely doing what was expected of me. So I chose to exercise this unexpected power in the only way that truly made it my choice – I gave the thumbs down, to general gasps of astonishment. So Beric died undeservedly. No wonder we didn't get on too well!

But that's not the end of this story! Many years later I went with my husband and son, then an older teenager, to visit Chesters Roman Fort on Hadrian's Wall. We each wandered around alone and afterwards compared notes.

Keith had felt he was there when the place was still being built, albeit some years after it had first been occupied, and he had been in charge of a platoon of soldiers doing some of the building. I felt that I had been a high class courtesan who was used by the officer-in-charge to even up the numbers at official feasts, and to discreetly entertain visiting VIPs. Both Keith and another man I knew at the time in this life, also a ranking soldier then, loved me and wanted to marry me, but I had no intention of giving up my life of luxury and ease to become a hard-working wife of a soldier. Keith took this philosophically, but the other man didn't - he could not understand how I could prefer not to be made an honest woman of, and became embittered and resentful.

One day I was invited to dine with a top visiting officer of the Roman Empire, who turned out to be Beric. Not surprisingly, given the previous life recounted above, he treated me like dirt. There was nothing I could do about it as I would have jeopardised my place at the Fort – I had to just sit there and take it.

Beric experienced precognition at various times, usually trivial things, like seeing our draining board unusually empty except for a sponge, which actually happened some time later. This is often called 'deja vue' (already seen).

The first one he remembers was when he was 19 and had recently bought his first car, a red VW Beetle. We were driving to our first Vegan Camp in July 1991, which was in North Wales, with Keith and me in our car, being followed by Beric and his sister in his Beetle. At some point along this unfamiliar route Keith went the wrong way, whilst Beric turned correctly right. He remembered 'seeing' this exact scene before he had even bought the Beetle – the layout of the roads, the view of the inside of the vehicle as he looked across his sister in the passenger seat at us…

He had a similar experience in his next vehicle, a VW 'splittie', again having the precognition before he had acquired the vehicle.

The only memory I have of our daughter that could possibly be classed as paranormal was when she was about three years old. She often said, "when I'm a Mummy" when what she really meant was "when I'm grown up". She had said, "When I'm a Mummy I'm going to drive a lorry", to which I replied, "Oh no you're not. When you're a Mummy you'll have to stay at home and look after your baby". After a few moments of thought she said, "When I'm a Mummy I'm going to drive a lorry - you can stay at home and look after the baby"!

One day I asked her if she knew how she'd become a Mummy. Her clear and instantaneous response was "Yes, six soldiers". Well, yes, that would do it! If that's a memory of a previous life then I'm very glad that she's forgotten it!

I am very proud of both my children, who have grown up to be very sensible and responsible adults who are both very good at listening to people and helping them with their problems.

Our Involvement With Spiritualism

Keith taking a service at Surrey Street, 2002.

We first attended several services at Grosvenor Road Spiritualist Church, St. Paul's, Bristol. The first service we went to, in August 1971, was taken by Mr George Ellis who gave the entire address with his eyes shut. It was probably a very good, spiritual, address, as I got to know him later as an excellent medium and healer. However, this first time, I couldn't stop wondering why he had his eyes shut, and so barely listened to his talk. We were, unusually, greeted at the door by a black man, who also bid us goodbye afterwards. It was a friendly church and we went several times. However, we had determined to visit all the churches in Bristol to see which we liked best.

The second church we visited was going to be Bishop Street (now closed) but what we hadn't realised was that the street had been cut in half by a new building and we only found the wrong half. That day we ended up at Surrey Street, also in St Paul's (and also now closed) but the next week we found the right place. We liked it there, they welcomed us warmly, and so it was a long time before we went anywhere else.

By October 1972 we were both on the committee - I was Membership Secretary and Assistant Leader of the Ladies Guild, and Keith was Vice-President! (I was the only one who had not voted for him at the AGM as I thought we were both too inexperienced for such a position).

I was soon running the weekday Guild, and we were attending many local meetings of the S.N.U. (Spiritualists' National Union) as Class A and Class B members, (representing the church, and as individuals).

The SNU promotes knowledge of the religion and philosophy of Spiritualism. They unite Spiritualists throughout the world and support Spiritualist societies and churches who share the following Seven Principles.

- The Fatherhood of God.
- The Brotherhood of Man.
- The Communion of Spirits and the Ministry of Angels.
- The Continuous Existence of the human soul.
- Personal Responsibility.
- Compensation and Retribution hereafter for all the good and evil deeds done on earth.
- Eternal Progress open to every human soul.

We stayed with Bishop Street Church until the President told us that some of the members had complained of the noise our young children made at the services. They really weren't making much noise, and I'd always asked the mediums if they minded having them there, and they'd all said "no, that's fine".

Usually at the Guild meetings on the Tuesday afternoons one of us sat at the back with the children, with colouring books etc, while the other chaired. On Sundays we usually both sat with them.

I remember one Sunday service taken by Mrs Carrie Bugden-Williams that Keith chaired – I was hemmed in by someone else, when our son, hearing his father's voice, crawled under the chairs and all the way down the aisle to the front, climbing the two steps to the rostrum, having never climbed any steps before, and spent the rest of the service in his father's arms, much to the delight of all present. However, you cannot stop young children making some noise, so I felt I had to stop going.

At that time Keith was Vice-President still and very involved in the running of the church, particularly ferrying mediums to and from the services. On the other hand I was growing increasingly resentful of the fact that I was denied the opportunity to do what we both wanted to do, and that now he was the only one able to. When the next AGM was looming I tried to persuade him to stand down, but he wasn't listening to me, and every time I tried to raise the subject we went off at a tangent and ended up arguing about something entirely different. He had put his name forward to stand again and I knew that I could not take another year of that. I was at my wits end. I could not get him to understand! Eventually I decided to write him a letter setting out how I felt. I left the letter on the table for him to find in the morning, with a note on it saying to open it when he had time to read and digest it.

He was working for BOC Transhield at the time, delivering foods to Marks and Spencer, and started work at any time between 1 and 5 a.m., a job he did for almost eight years, from 1971-79. He read the letter then and there, and subsequently withdrew his name from the election. That is the only time that our marriage was ever threatened.

We were sitting by then in a church circle run by a natural medium and the leader of the Ladies Guild, Mrs Carrie Ellis, who had only discovered when she was 17 that not everyone can see spirit. By then she was attending services at Bristol's first Spiritualist Church, Surrey Street, and one day the booked medium did not arrive. Everyone was in a flap about what to do, so she said "But anyone can do that!" That's when she learnt they couldn't!

The circle met weekly and you were expected to attend every week come hell or high water. The development of psychic and spiritual gifts needs commitment and dedication. Over many months of sitting in her circle, we slowly learnt many interesting things about her and about matters psychic and spiritual. We learnt discipline, which is of paramount importance. When we started to get spirit drawing close to us and trying to control us, we learnt that you must control your controls. In other words, you are in control and you can allow spirit to work with and through you or not as you please, which means that you also have to exercise discrimination regarding which spirits you allow through, and under what circumstances.

There are different levels of control. Control is the term used when another being (spirit) takes control of a mediums' voice-box, and sometimes his or her whole body. This can happen when clairvoyance or healing is given, and is especially useful when spirit teachings are given, as the words can then be more accurately conveyed. If it is not done with permission, then it is called possession. Beings from the higher realms will never do it without permission.

At the deepest level, the medium is unaware of what is happening, so has to be told afterwards what was said and done through her or him. This is also called 'deep trance', and can be dangerous to the medium if suddenly interrupted.

At a lighter level, the mediums' spirit just steps aside and so is aware of what the control is saying and doing, but does not interfere. This is also called 'light trance'. At this level it is possible for the medium to cut the connection at will. It can also be accidentally cut by outside occurrences, but with little or no danger to the medium.

Both Keith and I decided that we always wanted to know what was happening, so we only ever allowed light control.

The first gift we began to develop was that of healing, for which it is useful to also have a degree of clairvoyance.

Clairvoyance strictly speaking means simply 'clear seeing' and does not need an ability to communicate with spirit, or even to be psychic. It means that you are able to see situations for what they are, not what you or others would like them to be, and therefore you are able to accept whatever is, and give wise advice. This is also known as 'claircognisance'. However, the word 'clairvoyance' is more generally used to mean seeing things that others can't, i.e. psychically. Even more generally it is used to cover other psychic abilities such as clairaudience (clear hearing) and clairsentience (clear sensing). None of these abilities denote spirituality, as they can be used for good or ill depending on who is using them. Nor do they require mediumship, which is the ability to channel messages and/or teachings from the spirit world, either directly (when in trance) or indirectly.

I sat in the Bishop Street circle until I was pregnant with my first baby - I wasn't told to stop sitting but I knew. When sitting in a circle it is advisable never to arrive shortly after a very full meal – it makes you feel rather peculiar, a bit dizzy and light-headed. When I was about three months pregnant that's how I felt, so I knew I had to stop for the duration of the pregnancy. However, not wishing to miss out on the after-circle discussion, I would sit at the back of the church while the others sat, and then join them afterwards.

I didn't know how I knew, but I was sure I was carrying a boy and I wouldn't buy anything pink. In due course I gave birth to my first-born – a boy. Before I became pregnant again, two years later, I knew that my next baby would be a girl, and so it was. Having decided to stop at two children we had not chosen another name 'just in case' (as we had the first time). I remember my mother asking what we were going to call the new baby, and saying, "what if it's a boy?"

"It won't be a boy" I said.
"But what if it is?" insisted my mother.

"Well, we'll call it Frank or something", I said, just to keep her happy. (Remember, this was well before the introduction of ultra-scans.)

In the maternity home when I had just given birth to my daughter I asked the nurse if he was all right, then immediately corrected myself to 'she'. She looked at me curiously and said, "How do you know that? I haven't told you yet!"

Our daughter's naming service at Bishop Street church, conducted by George and Carrie Ellis

I remember that whilst sitting quietly in the Bishop Street circle, we would become aware of the steady tick-tock of a wall clock – not the one that was there then, which was battery-operated and made no noise – but the sound of the big old school clock Mrs Ellis said used to be there.

In June 1976, soon after we had withdrawn from the church, the circle moved into the home of Mr and Mrs Ellis.

Being a life-long natural psychic she had lots of tales to tell, some of which might have frightened weaker souls (actually I think that was the idea, as it takes quite a strong soul to develop psychic powers safely). Soon after she had realised not all people had her gifts, she tried an experiment. The committee room of Surrey Street Church had at that time a very heavy wooden table in it. One day when she was in there on her own, she decided to see if she could move it psychically. She told us that it lifted into the air, moved across the room and came to rest in a different place. It took four men to carry it back to where it had been, and she was told off in no uncertain terms by the leaders of the church, as it had drained all the psychic energy from the entire building!

Another time she told us of a woman who had been brought to them one Friday, who was addicted to the 'glass'. She wouldn't do anything without first asking the 'glass' if it was alright – not even go to the shops. Consequently she had attracted numerous entities around her, which were doing her no good. Mrs Ellis told us she and her husband spent three hours clearing the woman of these entities, and before she left they warned her not to touch the 'glass' again or she would end up in Barrow Gurney (the local mental home) on the Monday. Apparently she had gone straight home and asked the 'glass' if what had happened had been okay – by the Monday she was in Barrow Gurney.

She also told us of the time she had become aware, as she slept, of having a baby placed in her arms. She said it felt like holding cobwebs and she knew it had just died. It had been given to her to comfort. As she realised these things she heard a voice say, "she's aware" - whereupon she abruptly awoke. She believed she was not meant to know about this, and if they hadn't realised in time that she had become aware of what was happening then she may have seen too much and would not have been allowed to return to her earth life – she would have been found dead in bed with no explanation.

We also became acquainted with an old lady who had attended Grosvenor Road Church for a great many years, and who had sat in circle for forty years, during which time she had never had any psychic experiences herself, but was happy to be the 'battery' that helped others to develop. She told us of the many times she had attended materialisation séances at the church – something that rarely happens these days. This is where the medium allows herself, or himself, to be used by spirits who wish to actually, physically, appear to their loved ones. They take from the medium a substance called ectoplasm and mould it around their features, and sometimes their whole body, thus making themselves visible (and, with permission, touchable on occasions).

This was in the days when there was a lot of controversy about this, and accusations of fraud, so the mediums would be subjected to strict examinations beforehand. Our friend, Mrs Martin, was one of the ladies of the church who would be present as the female medium undressed, allowed herself to be searched – including in all her orifices – and would be dressed in a simple robe. She would then be led to a specially prepared and searched cabinet which had a curtain across the front, where she would sit on a chair in a dim red light, sometimes with arms and legs strapped to the chair.

I particularly remember being told of one occasion when there was an interruption to the proceedings and consequently the ectoplasm rushed back to the medium far too quickly (which can cause severe health problems for the medium, as indeed happened in the famous case of Helen Duncan, who had suffered many burns to her body from the ectoplasm returning too quickly, and who died in 1956 after five weeks in hospital following a similar occasion). What fascinated me the most was being told by Mrs Martin that she had seen with her own eyes, after having previously examined the medium, the debris from the floor, drawn up with the ectoplasm, which had been deposited on the medium, including a drawing pin that had ended up under her armpit!

We had started by developing as channels for healing which led naturally to us also developing as channels for spirit, i.e. mediums. Having been distracted from various addresses by mediums speaking with their eyes closed, as previously noted, or by those who channelled spirit in a distinctly different voice, especially a female medium speaking with a male voice so low that it sounded painful, I decided that I would not do those things. Our circle leader, Mrs Ellis, had told us early on that we needed to 'control our controls' and not allow them to run our lives, or intrude when not wanted. Therefore we developed our mediumship, at least in public, with eyes open and using our own voices.

The latter - speaking using our own voices - has mostly continued, but I have had to allow the former - shutting my eyes - as eventually I found that to not do so hindered my contact with spirit helpers from the higher realms. They were finding it increasingly distracting trying to give a talk whilst looking through my eyes. Having been in the spirit world for so long they had grown unaccustomed to seeing things as we see them, instead seeing people in terms of energy and colour. I have compromised by explaining this from time to time if I feel that there are those in the congregation/audience who might not understand, as I had not, and miss the actual content of the talk.

As to the voice, I have found that sometimes I need to be so strongly controlled to begin with that the voice is not mine, but that as the talk progresses the control can ease off and so my own voice reappears.

I also found it necessary to ban spirit from our bedroom unless invited, or in an emergency. This arose from those times early on when, laying quietly in bed at night before going to sleep, I would say something to Keith and find I was answered through him by someone else! Once our spirit friends know what we want, they are very good at going along with our wishes – in fact, they are not allowed by Divine Law to do otherwise.

In private we were sometimes controlled by spirits who brought through some of their own characteristics including their voice. A particular favourite was an Irish tinker who introduced himself as Shaun O'Rafferty and his wife as Shelagh, and told us of the times when they travelled around Britain in a horse-drawn caravan selling their wares. Shaun always makes us laugh, but his wife is much quieter and more serious, and did try to do automatic writing through me, with some success eventually - but I didn't keep that up.

Automatic writing is where the hand of the medium is controlled, allowing spirit to directly write on the paper. It can also be used to allow your own sub-conscious through, usually more in the form of absent-minded doodles than writing.

Another visiting spirit I remember was an Indian brave who totally controlled me as I sat and then stood up in a very dignified fashion, folded his arms high in front of him, and then was taken aback when they would not lower as far as he was expecting them to onto his (my) chest! Sometimes Keith would appear taller than usual, at other times he appeared like a small wizened old man. I remember once opening my eyes too soon after being used as a channel at home and feeling surprised that I was not six inches taller!

Another psychic sense I experienced occasionally was that of smell – pipe smoke, which I associated with my late Uncle Jack; lilies-of-the-valley (my mother-in-law); hyacinths on our landing, at the wrong time of year; apple pie, when none was being baked ...

We thought that our departure from Bishop Street Church would be the end of our association with Spiritualism until the children were grown up – but not a bit of it! Within six months we had been asked to help run another church.

Around that time there had been a great to-do centred on Grosvenor Road Church that was in all the papers, local and national. The Secretary of that church had publicly accused Mr Gordon Higginson, the President of the Spiritualists' National Union, of cheating when he had taken a service there. The other members of the committee had disagreed and had all resigned in protest. This led to another election of a committee, but due to a technicality the only valid nomination for secretary was the same lady – so again, all the others resigned, leaving the SNU no option but to close the church.

However, a leading member of that church, who was also well known to the national leaders, offered to re-open the church with her as caretaker and to run it until such time as a committee could be re-formed. This was agreed, and she asked Keith and me to help her. As Grosvenor Road had a vestry with a very thick wall where one of us could sit with the children while the other chaired the services, we accepted. Even if the children did make a lot of noise (which they never had before), they would not have been heard in the church. We took it in turns to do this. We thought this arrangement would last for about six months, but we ran that church, with Mrs Oscroft overseeing, for 18 months before it was closed with dignity, and sold.

It was during this time that we became certified healers with the Guild of Spiritualist Healers – Keith first because the application had to be signed by the Secretary of the Church, which was me, and I didn't feel able to sign my own application.

Also during this time I was present as minute-taker at one of the meetings in the church when Mr Higginson met his accuser. He had come from the North, Stoke-on-Trent I believe, and had been inhospitably left alone for some time in the church prior to the service. His accuser alleged that during that time he had memorised the list of members and their photos (I never saw a church with photos of their members!) and had then used this information to give messages at the service. Utter rubbish! In any case, he of all people didn't need to stoop to such depths.

Much later I saw him take a service at Bedminster Spiritualist Church, when it was at Hebron Road. As I did not like looking up at the mediums through the white and blue painted ironwork, I sat alone in the gallery. The wonderful organ was up behind the rostrum and that evening was being played by Ron Fudge, who lived not far from us in our village. During the evening Gordon Higginson turned his back on us all and spoke to Ron. He told him the number of his house, the name of the road and the village (well almost, *Oldham* Common instead of *Oldland* Common – an understandable mistake for a Northerner) and described his father to him. He said that Ron's father was telling him that he had been with Ron that morning when he had gone for a walk around a new housing estate. All of which was confirmed by Ron. However when Gordon said that the name of the road that Ron had been in was called Pennine something, Ron could not confirm that as he did not know. The name signs had not yet been put up. I must have been the only one there who knew that Gordon was right, as I had seen it in the local freebie newspaper, and also on the electoral roll. Impressive!

After Grosvenor Road was closed a few of the members met weekly in the home of Mrs Chisholm. We still had assets, and were looking for somewhere else to use as a church.

Eventually we found the right place at Hillfields. We hired the Community Centre hall on Thicket Avenue for Sunday services, and called ourselves the Aquarian United Spiritualist Church. Gordon Higginson took our first service. Mrs Chisholm was President, and insisted that Roy Rowsell be Vice-President (apparently he wouldn't come on the committee as anything else). I was Secretary, and Keith was an ordinary committee member, as was our friend Alf Wilcox, whom I had known as a child as he lived at the bottom of our road, and was known by my parents.

My parents had met when they played piano and violin in the local Folk House Orchestra back in 1927, and my Dad also played a trombone. Alf played a trumpet in a brass band, and Dad would sometimes help them out. I had been a little scared of Alf as a child, as he had a large lump beside one eye, and he had always seemed so stern to me. I'd never talked to him until I found that he was a member of Grosvenor Road Church, but since then he had become a good friend with whom we'd had lots of fun.

One person who joined the church later used to think it was awful the way Alf treated me – the things he said - and despite her inbred respect for older people, wondered how I took it so quietly. Then one day she was present when I got my own back and she realised that I could give as good as I got!

He used to tell us of the practical jokes he had played. He used to work at Masson Scott Thrissell, at Easton, an engineering works. In the Depression, like so many others, he was out of work. He may have been able to get work if he had been prepared to take less than the Union rate, but he was a Union man and stuck to his principles. He traipsed around Bristol trying to find work day after day. One day he was walking home from town at the end of another long and fruitless search when he heard a voice in his head telling him to go and ask at Thrissell's. He said, "but I've been there already – there's no work". But the voice insisted, so he went and asked again. The Manager said, "how did you know I had a vacancy? It's only just happened". That's how he got the job at Thrissell's. He worked there for the rest of his working life, being put in charge of women workers during the war as most of the men joined up. He probably wasn't fit enough. He'd had a hernia since the age of 23, as well as that growth over his eye. He was terrified of hospitals, but that's another story.

First I want to tell you of some of his practical jokes, mostly I think from before the war:

You can imagine that in the 1930s life was hard, and each Christmas the works ran a raffle for a turkey. Alf"s gang told this man that he had won. He went home and told his wife, who of course was delighted. But the rotten lot stuffed a sausage skin with dung and shaped it to look like a turkey. I believe it was the day before Christmas Eve when they presented him with this - inside a shoe-box and wrapped up in brown paper. He took it home in all good faith, but when his missus opened it she naturally was furious and berated him in no uncertain terms, poor man.

Another time a man brought a brand new bicycle to work, but when he went to go home he found it had been painted in all different colours.

Then there were the more harmless pranks of sending a new boy to buy a tin of elbow grease, or a left-handed screwdriver.

One time a manager they didn't like had a new overall. The next morning when he went to put it on he couldn't – someone had stitched up the sleeves.

And we go on about today's youth! But I think I may have paid him back for all those hapless victims.

We got on tremendously well, and we could talk for hours on the phone, but for some reason he didn't like my eyes – they made him feel uncomfortable, as if he was back at school with a stern Headmistress. At committee meetings he would say very little, and always looked at me to see what I wanted saying or doing. He had the greatest respect and admiration for me, and always backed me up. Very flattering, and very useful, especially combined with the fact that if I looked at him when he was talking he would dry up!

After we had established the church at Hillfields, our children being aged about five and seven, our daughter, the youngest, would sometimes get up on stage during or after the service and sing something she had learned at school. One of us would be chairing, whilst the other usually sat with the children at the back of the hall where they could colour or read and move quietly about without distracting anyone. This particular day Beric sat with Alf at the back, while his sister sat with me at the front ready to go on stage. Just before the service started I realised that I had left her cuddly toy at the back so I walked back to get it. Part way there I noticed that Alf was looking at me apprehensively. So I put on my sternest expression and headed straight for him. By the time I reached him he was cowering in his seat! I didn't say a word, just reached over him to get the toy and turned away. He told Keith it took him the rest of the service to recover!

Aquarian United Church fancy dress party, Dec 1980

After the services Keith would go on stage behind the curtains, with others, and give healing to anyone who wanted it. I preferred to stay in the body of the hall to talk to people. We served tea and biscuits, so many people stayed. Released from having to be so still and quiet, our children would enjoy the freedom of the hall – although still not allowed to make too much noise. On one such occasion I was engaged in conversation with some new people when I saw Beric across the other side of the hall doing something he should not have been doing. Unwilling to leave these people, I tried to catch his eye with a warning look, with no success of course as he was too absorbed in what he was doing. I had not noticed that Alf had been between us until I saw him move towards a chair – he had intercepted my look and wondered what he had done to upset me. His legs turned to jelly and he had to sit down!

We had a blue minibus at that time that we used to ferry people around. We got into the habit of giving Alf two rings on the phone, which signalled that we were about to leave home, so we would be picking him up in about 20 minutes. You remember I said he lived on the same road that I grew up on – well one time we rang him from my parents' house and so could be with him in about two minutes! Our friend Charlie was with him for tea that day, as luck would have it, and witnessed this. Alf heard the rings and told Charlie that Keith and Helen would be there in 20 minutes, and then went upstairs to change. When we appeared two minutes later at the door he was still in his vest!

His hernia was causing him problems, and we kept on at him to see a doctor, not nagging but jokingly. He told us he had only ever let his wife see his hernia by pulling down the top of his pyjama trousers just enough. One day we had been out somewhere with him and Charlie, and on the way back had decided to have some fun, with a serious purpose (we knew he had to get over his fear of hospitals) and so had stopped outside of the General Hospital so that, we told him, he could get that hernia seen to. I had made an effort to get him out of the back, physically trying to pull him out. He said later that if I had not given up when I did he would not have had the strength to resist the pull any longer. As a result he always carried enough money with him to get a taxi home if ever he got caught out, as he knew if he had called us out to rescue him we would have taken him straight to a hospital. Eventually he saw the sense of our arguments and went to see his doctor. He was admitted to hospital to have both his hernia and the growth above his eye operated on. A nurse told him, "leave your modesty at the door and collect it on the way out". At long last he had overcome his fear of hospitals! The operations were a success, but as this had been the last thing he had to do on this earth he was shortly afterwards granted his most cherished wish, which was to join his 'missus' in the next world.

I still miss him - we had such fun together! It's never been the same since he passed over.

We worked hard for this church, booking the mediums, sometimes picking them up, setting out the hall, chairing the services and, after the service, Keith would go on stage behind the curtain and join others to give healing, whilst I remained on the floor of the hall talking to people, as previously mentioned – all this at the same time as bringing up the children. We had others who would serve refreshments and help clear up. We would also ferry people to and from the hall. And, of course, I did the minutes of the meetings. We tried to get others to chair the services sometimes as we consider it very good training if anyone is aiming to become a speaker and/or demonstrator. Most people have to learn to throw their voices, and sometimes to slow their speech down, as it doesn't matter how good the address or the clairvoyance if people in the room cannot hear and understand it.

It would also have been good to sit back and enjoy the service, or to have a break now and then, and to know that the church was in capable hands.

After a while Roy became President, but Keith and I continued doing most of the work. After only a couple of years we found it was too much, as we were getting so little help from others, so we resigned. We were later told that people thought we didn't want help, as they understood that we wanted all the power to ourselves! If only they had told us that before we felt pushed into resigning! It would seem that whoever started that rumour was the one who actually wanted the power!

Less than a year later, in 1983, they found an old Catholic chapel for sale on Soundwell Road, which is still functioning as a Spiritualist Church.

It was in 1988 that we transferred our allegiance from the S.N.U.'s Guild of Spiritualist Healers to the World Federation of Healers. This followed the way the S.N.U. had handled complaints about the Leader of the Healing Group at that church – or rather mis-handled it in our view. There had been several complaints laid at this persons' door by different people. We knew two people very well, who were then attending the church and helping out, who kept us informed of what was happening. We would have expected that, pending investigation, the Leader of the Healing Group would have been suspended from that position, but this did not happen, and the whole investigation seemed to us to be a whitewash.

Since then we have largely steered clear of any involvement with an individual church, whilst at the same time working in many of them. The one exception was when I was asked to run a meditation group for a local church, which I still run even though that church has now closed.

PART TWO

Different aspects of the paranormal.

"At the very frontier of science new ideas are emerging that challenge everything we believe about how our world works and how we define ourselves."

"Through scientific experiment they'd *[quantum physicists]* demonstrated that there may be such a thing as a life force flowing through the universe – what has variously been called collective consciousness or, as theologians have termed it, the Holy Spirit. They provided a plausible explanation of all those areas that over the centuries mankind has had faith in but no solid evidence of or adequate accounting for, from the effectiveness of alternative medicine and even prayer to life after death, They offered us, in a sense, a science of religion."

Lynne McTaggart
"The Field" 2003

Residual Energies

Me in Oldland valley, 1982

Residual energy is the name given to those energies of a person or event that remain with the buildings and objects that they were connected to on earth. It is this energy that is used in psychometry - the term used when psychics and mediums receive images from such objects or buildings.

It can also remain with the land after battles and similar dramatic and emotional happenings. I'm told that at Auschwitz former concentration camp no flowers grow and no birds sing, such was the horror of events there during the Second World War.

Many of the presences felt in houses are not spirits at all, but the ghosts of times past – an echo of former people, identifiable by the fact that one cannot interact with them. They will slowly fade over time, depending on how strong they are in the first place, and how strong have been the energies since. This natural process can be speeded up by overlaying the previous energies with others – like rubbing out a chalk drawing, and doing another one on the same board.

When we first bought our house, back in 1970, I used to walk around the neighbourhood getting to know it. One day I walked along the valley and came to a privately-owned cutting in the rock that was rather inadequately fenced off, but that I knew had once been a dramway - a railway where horses hauled trucks, usually loaded with coal.

Being curious to see the cutting, I cautiously entered and slowly moved along, treading carefully over the stony ground. As I turned a corner and so was hidden from sight, I relaxed a little and began to tune into the atmosphere of this place. It was a beautiful little world of towering rocks, plants and wildlife – a rabbit had looked at me curiously for a moment before disappearing. I continued along and, much to my surprise, found myself feeling more apprehensive with every step, until an urgent fear began to rise up within me. Puzzling over this, I found myself visualising a straggly line of dowdily-dressed women, many with headscarves, urging young children to go faster, whilst trying not to communicate to them the real fear that they felt. As I continued to walk forward this feeling got stronger and stronger, until I really had to fight against it. I also shared their fear that the ground they were walking on might be mined. By this time I could see the end of the cutting – a tunnel which was now barred with wire netting, but which was obviously the destination of these women. I determined to walk right up to this tunnel entrance, but found the fear emanating from it too strong and so stopped a few feet short.

Later I visited the parish church and looked at a collage display there made by local children, showing the history of the area. The one that drew my attention illustrated the Second World War, showing how civilians took shelter from the bombers in the very tunnel I had seen.

Relating this to an historian friend of mine later, he told me that some of the local railway lines had indeed been mined, though never that one. Of course, those WWII women would not have known that, and so their fear would have been real, and their joint emotions were so powerful that they had left their mark in that cutting - and were still powerful because there had been few people there since.

Some time later I took a clairvoyant friend there, without telling him why, to see if he could pick up the same as I had, but he touched the rocks alongside and tuned into the time when it had all been primeval forest!

Many people respond to residual energies without realising it, so do not know that their depression or anger or timidity or whatever are not really theirs, and so can be eliminated. In the same way, some people will pick up other people's complaints, such as headaches, without realising, much as Keith did when he was young, when he would find himself imitating people's limps. When this happens to us now, even if we are not certain whether it is ours or not, we ask that healing be sent to whoever it belongs to and the condition be taken away from us.

Many years ago I knew a young man of 23 who could not go into the centre of town because of this – he would pick up everyone's ailments and emotions and return home a jangled mess. It is for this reason that one is advised to 'close down' after 'opening up' to do spiritual work, whether it be healing, clairvoyance, meditation or whatever. When you help others you 'open up' your heart automatically and your energies flow out of you, or, hopefully, through you, so afterwards you need to 'close down' these channels so that the flow is not reversed, causing you to start picking up other people's energies instead. Some people also 'close down' automatically, but if you are not one of them then you need to intentionally seal off these channels of energy flow by one of a number of means - the simplest being to imagine yourself flinging a beautiful blue floor-length cloak around you, and pulling the hood over your head, or maybe picturing a golden cone dropping around you.

I have written some suggestions to help you in Part Three of this book.

I found I had to be careful when buying second-hand items – once I bought a lovely hand-knitted sweater, which I found I did not feel happy in when I first wanted to wear it to a Spiritualist Church – the previous owner would not have approved!

Although it is not only second-hand items one needs to be wary of. When I was younger I rode a motorbike, and after some time found that my elbows were playing up a bit when it was cold, so I bought a pair of elbow-warmers. I realised after a while that every time I wore them I ended up tearful, so I psychometrised them. I found that in the packing plant after they were made, there was a pile of them which a worker had leant upon while she poured out her heart to a colleague – and all her sorrow had been absorbed by that pile of elbow-warmers.

On both of these occasions I then cleared them of these vibrations, and substituted my own.

Mind you, it is entirely possible that old items could have their former owners attached to them! We were called to a house once where voices were heard upstairs when no-one was there. We found two ladies bickering in a room full of second-hand clothes! They had come with some of the clothes, didn't get on, and couldn't understand what they were doing there. Needless to say, we helped them cross over.

I remember when I first started as a volunteer at the Sir Bernard Lovell School, our local secondary school (at which my son had recently started), helping out the history teacher who had been newly appointed to be the school's Librarian. Having had considerable experience in libraries I was especially helpful to him and we worked on an extended Dewey scheme to classify his large collection of newspaper and magazine articles, postcards, pieces of clay pipe and other tactile items. One day, when I had arranged to work with him on this in one of his spare periods, I arrived to find that he had been asked to stand in for an absent teacher. I found myself sitting with him in front of this class who were doing work set by their usual teacher, but every now and again had to be quietened and re-directed to their task. It was a double period, so I think it lasted one and a half hours. During that time we had our heads together quietly going over my proposals and his requirements. On the way home at lunchtime I felt totally drained, as if I had done a day's hard labour. This took me by surprise, as it had been quite a restful and pleasant time. It took me the rest of the day to recover, by which time I had worked out that, as we had worked so closely together in total harmony, my energy must have been drawn out of me and into him, in the same way that water will find its own level. He had been "chasing his tail" for weeks since his summer holiday appointment to the job of Librarian, and through this new school year, and so hadn't been sleeping well, having so much on his mind. He wasn't expecting me but I decided to go and see him the next day just to confirm my suspicions. I found him full of beans having had the best night's sleep that he'd had in a long time! After that I was more careful around him, not minding him taking some of my energy, but being careful to leave enough for me.

Going through my mother's things after her passing I found lots of letters – she was a great letter-writer, and a hoarder. Reading through a particular hand-written letter, I suddenly realised that it was the original letter her mother had received telling of my grandfather's death in 1916 on the battlefields of France. As this realisation hit me, I found myself sobbing great gulping sobs such as I have never experienced in my life! I really felt as my grandmother must have felt all those years ago on first reading that letter.

At a healing event in Wedmore, Somerset, I was relaxing with my sandwiches in the shade on a beautiful sunny day, when I got into conversation with a man. He discovered that I was a healer and a medium, and when his daughter's friend joined us the conversation had just gotten around to psychometry. This friend didn't know what this was, so he told her to give me something of hers to hold. She took off a pendant that hung around her neck, and I was suddenly faced with having to 'perform'.

I duly tuned in and began describing a woman who had owned the pendant before her. I was told that this was true, and that it had been given to her by this friend. I was describing a tall thin woman, not very old, and I said that she wasn't interested in fashion as clothes hung on her like she was a tent pole. I realised what I had said and began apologising for being so blunt and even rude – I was horrified at the way I had phrased this! But they were laughing, and they said that I was exactly right and that she knew this and wouldn't have minded. Phew!

On a relatively new housing estate near to us a friend had recently moved into one of the houses - one which had lain empty for some time since the previous residents had left and had then been re-decorated and altered a bit by her landlord and his wife. I was asked to give it the once-over psychically first. I had never been in such a blank-feeling house – it had no atmosphere from the past at all, except a slight warmth in one bedroom. For some months after moving in with her young son she didn't feel at home, even though she had added many touches of her own to the décor, so I advised her to invite friends and family round for a house-warming party. The preparations, socialising and best wishes engendered began to add that certain something that had been lacking. Other such occasions have continued the process.

Helping Souls Cross Over

Me and Keith, 1996

Our first experience of clearing houses had happened in the early 1980s. The husband of a fellow Spiritualist called us in after his wife had left him, taking their youngest with her, but leaving the other children with him. She had delved far deeper than us into the mysteries of life and had become obsessed with all things occult. Consequently she had developed what I call 'mental indigestion', and, worse, had been drawn into things better left alone. Her husband felt the house needed clearing of the presences she had encouraged, and also wanted to stop her bringing anything back in when she visited. We were not his first choice – he had asked a very experienced medium, who had declined on the grounds that he felt it would be beyond him. (It is wise to have two of you at least on such occasions and far better to decline than to take risks). So we went in where angels feared to tread!

After previously preparing ourselves and asking for help and protection, we carefully covered the whole house, including the attic and all cupboards, bit by bit, bringing in the white purifying light. We knew that she considered that we did not have the power to do this, or to block her, and we didn't know if she was right – but we did it because her husband knew no-one else who would, and neither did we.

To stop her bringing back in any lower forces we finished by putting up a curtain of light at both of the outside doors with the intention of preventing any dark spirit from entering. The husband later told us that on her next visit she didn't stay long and seemed uncomfortable there.

Not long afterwards we were called to a house in Mangotsfield, near Bristol, to find out about a recurring psychic phenomenon. The house was two old miners' cottages knocked into one. The problem was that, on occasions, the bedcovers in one of the bedrooms would be tugged at whilst the bed was occupied. That was all – and the owners were not worried by this, but when this happened whilst a young American man was visiting it frightened him so much he went straight back home! (And I thought Americans liked ghosts!).

We quickly made contact with an old lady who in the latter years of her life had been confined to that room by failing health. She had been looked after by her husband until he fell down the stairs, and passed on as a result of this. She had seen him lying there but had been unable to get down to him. Her neighbours had subsequently looked after her. This had been about 70 years before. She had never had to think for herself as she had always done what men had told her to, first her father, then brothers, husband and priest. When it was her turn to pass on she did not know what to do, as no-one had told her. So she was trying to get someone's attention by pulling at the covers! We introduced her to some of our spirit friends and told her to go with them. She did, and that's the last we heard.

Soon after, we were called to a house on a post-war estate at Hillfields, Bristol. Their young child had become disturbed by something in the bedroom. We found (in spirit) an elderly couple there looking after their lively grandson, who was the one causing the problems, probably through boredom. For instance, the small table at the foot of the stairs would sometimes be found at the top instead. The woman was unwilling to go at first, fearing that the three of them would be separated, so we asked our spirit friends to bring someone she knew. Soon she was exclaiming delightedly at seeing an old friend again and then gladly agreed to go with our friends.

Keith then sent out thoughts asking if there was anyone else in the neighbourhood who needed help. We were amazed to find that there were lots of them. It appeared that in this old mining area they had relied on travelling preachers like John Wesley for their spiritual needs and had not seen one in many a long year. They crowded in, greeting each other as long-lost friends, and soon the atmosphere was like a party. They called Keith "the preacher-man".

Since then many of them have come back from time to time to help others in like situations, as part of our team.

We had a similar experience a few years later at a club in Kingswood. The manager and his sister had grown up in a house filled with friendly spirits, so the happenings at the club did not bother them, but the same could not be said for some of their staff and customers. We had visited their mother's house a few years previously in order to help any spirits that were earth-bound, as a result of which they called us in following the latest outbreak of phenomena.

The club was on the first floor of an old building that had previously been a *Tizer* drinks factory, and before that had been a boot and shoe factory – *G.B.Brittons*. Every Christmas when the decorations were brought out the phenomena would start – glasses moved about, lights switched on or off, cold areas in the bar ... The manager told us how, alone one evening, he had seen a ball of light speed down the corridor, violently push open the double doors, and disappear through the wall in front of them – that had once not been there.

When we were left alone in the main bar Keith was immediately taken over by a man who had Keith crying with relief – at last someone had come to talk to him! He was a Scot who had worked at the boot and shoe factory, and said his name was Arthur. After calming him down and introducing him to our spirit friends, we asked him if there were any others there in a similar situation. He said he had seen a young man, who was very shy. Between us we eventually managed to coax him out, and it transpired that he had been a general dogsbody and had been roughly treated, particularly by a woman they both called Mad Margaret. We established contact with her too – a large woman with red hair and a fiery temper.

We talked to them all for some time and got her to apologise to the boy for the way she had treated him. All this while, I was aware of being watched by a pipe-smoking old man seated against the wall in the L-shape of the room, who had seen it all before, but gradually realised this was different this time and so came over to join us. They were all so pleased at being helped at long last that they got Keith dancing on the dance floor!
Once again Keith sent out thoughts to see if there were any others around who needed help.

The room had double doors on the outside wall that had once been used to hoist goods in and out (remember that this was on the first floor). Keith felt loads of people coming in through these doors (no longer used, of course) pushing him back and back to the edge of the dance floor. Again a party atmosphere developed; and also again many of the souls we rescued that day have since come back to join our team when we seek to rescue others, either from being lost and earth-bound, or from the Darkness, where they have never known what love is.

In 1996 we were asked to visit a Victorian terraced house on Air Balloon Road, St. George, Bristol, where various things had happened. The new owners, a young couple, had builders in who had stripped the front downstairs room back to the stone walls and floor joists with the bare earth showing below. Not only had the builders heard footsteps whilst working alone in the room, but one morning an old coin from the 1930s had appeared on one of the joists – an old many-sided thrupenny bit, as I recall. Also a puppy got very distressed at night in certain rooms, and a friend had seen the form of a man in a room upstairs.

The thing that had made them call us in, however, was the presence at the top of the stairs, that the pregnant wife feared was about to push her down them. They knew that a man named Willie had died in the house, but we did not find him there. What we found was a 'lady of the house', wearing a long black dress with a high collar and with a sick adult son, Peter, who was confined to the downstairs front room (the one the builders had stripped bare) and who had died there, and a waif from a workhouse whom she had taken in. We also found another man, Dave, who was from a later time, and was still searching for something he had lost.

Having dealt with the adults, we then tracked the waif, called Tom, to the upstairs landing where he was hiding. He had not been well treated by the lady, having been worked hard and fed on crusts. We eventually persuaded him that he would be safe with the lady in blue who helps us on such occasions, and so he went with her to a better place.

All this didn't seem right for that house – a 'lady of the house' with a waif from a workhouse in a miner's cottage that was only a hundred years old? However, later investigation by the wife's mother-in-law revealed a manor house had once stood on that spot!

Two years later the wife reported that they hadn't had any more trouble since then.

Some years later we were called to an old vicarage on the outskirts of Bristol where the new owners were troubled by experiences they'd had since beginning restoration work inside. One of these experiences occurred when the lady was vacuuming in her jeans in one of the bedrooms. She felt that she was being watched disapprovingly by someone. In that room we found an old and ill woman, who was very reluctant to accept that she was 'dead'. She suffered from gout, which made her bad-tempered, and which death had not cured as she did not realise she *was* dead so had hung onto all her usual feelings. She was of the old school and disapproved of young women wearing trousers, hence the feeling related above. It wasn't until we managed to get her brother to appear that she believed us, and left.

There was also a vicar, who talked to me using Keith's voice box. He said his name was Paul, and that he had come to this place in, he thought, 1912. When further questioned he admitted that he did not know what year it was now. When I told him it was 2001 he put his (or more accurately Keith's) hand to his heart and said "Oh, bless me!" He was lovely, and when it had sunk in that he was what the world calls dead (a matter of seconds) he exclaimed, "No wonder the congregation aren't listening to me any more!"

When we told the ones who had asked for our help, the woman went a bit pale and said that she could swear that one of the names of past vicars in the church was Paul, and that it said 1912.

After Keith had spoken on a Radio Bristol phone-in, we were contacted by a farmer from Rangeworthy, near Bristol. He lived in a rambling old farmhouse, and his whole family turned out, as they had never met anyone like us and were fascinated. His teenage daughter had refused to sleep in her bedroom, so he sought our help. In that bedroom we found a young girl from a bygone era who felt that she had been abandoned by her parents. She was wearing a long everyday check dress in beige with smocking at the top. She meant no-one any harm, but was lonely. She went with our friends, and I hope the family have had no trouble since. In another (unused) room we found two boys and persuaded them to move on too. On the whole we felt that the place had been home to mainly happy souls.

Some years later we were invited by Radio Bristol to do a live broadcast from a house of their choosing. Here is an account by Keith about that Wednesday's interview at 116, Two Mile Hill. *"I moved into the corner of the room downstairs and linked in with the energy I felt there. The soul that was there impressed me with the name of George. When we were upstairs I managed to link in with an elderly lady (Jennifer) who had suffered a lot. I was picking up her condition, literally, with a bad breathing problem. I also picked up the tears that were with her, wanting her husband (George) so I told her I would bring him to her, so I went downstairs linked in with George and told him that I would take him to Jennifer. When we reached her, I felt an overwhelming feeling, as they were reunited, and with their tears that I was feeling. George had passed before Jennifer and they somehow had lost contact, possibly when she was moved away before she passed over. Having been in that room for a long time before she passed, she had returned to the place she knew."*

It's not easy doing this on radio as a lot of the time we are working in silence, telepathically, so as Keith worked I was trying to relate to the listeners what was happening.

The following week the presenter, Andy, rang the man who lived there asking how things were. He replied that since our visit there had been no more phenomena.

In December 2003 our daughter and her partner moved into their second house, which they quickly got into a sufficiently tidy state to entertain us, as usual, at Christmas.

They had an L-shaped living room, which had a concrete floor, only partially covered. Just by the door there was a tall narrow wooden book case, which had only a few ornaments and a small cactus on it. On the evening of Christmas Eve, we were all quietly sitting around chatting, me in a chair facing the door; Keith in a chair facing me; and the others on a settee in the other part of the L, from where they could not see the door. No-one was moving, either inside or outside the house, not even their cats and dog.

Suddenly I saw the bookcase beginning to tilt forwards, heading for the back of Keith's head! I didn't know what to do – if I said something Keith might look round and get it in his face instead. I had visions of us spending Christmas at a hospital with Keith with a fractured skull. A look of horror must have been on my face as everyone went silent, and Keith shifted slightly, preparing to turn around to see what I was looking at. It was just as well that he did as the bookcase hit him on the shoulder, just missing his head! It had all happened so quickly. The cactus landed in his lap!

When I realised that he was okay I began to laugh, which must have seemed rather heartless but was simply relief, and my way of releasing the tension and fear that I had been feeling. There was no reason we could see for this to have happened so later I tuned in to discover if this house had any unseen occupants. I became aware of an old and rather irate and bewildered woman, to whom I offered help to move on. Keith was unusually subdued that Christmas!

When we returned home after the New Year, we discovered that a patient of ours - an old lady, who had gone to spend Christmas at a holiday camp, instead of on her own - had been found dead in her bed there on Christmas Eve! I realised that the energies I had felt matched hers and I believe that she had somehow homed in on us, and had found herself in a strange house where everyone ignored her. No wonder she was bewildered and angry! I don't believe she meant us any harm, but was just trying to get our attention - she may have been simply trying to pick up something from a shelf. Being unused to the situation, she probably just used too much energy to do so and thus the whole bookcase came tumbling down.

On the 21st April 2004, Keith and I were called out urgently to a lady in Lockleaze, who was having problems with objects being moved, or disappearing. All the pens in her house had vanished, except for their tops; a small lampshade from a tealight had been thrown at her... She had been a Spiritualist for 30 years, and had been psychic since a child. These things had only begun to happen recently. When we arrived we found that the contents of an ornamental glass-topped table had been tipped onto the floor that morning – she had been sitting opposite and had seen it happen but could not move to try to stop it. It had held a lamp, which had broken, and a large heavy glass paperweight, which had not, also a load of glass pebbles and cubes. The top had been lifted off its suckers, yet the whole thing would have been very heavy.

We found that these things had been done by an officer from the Boer War days who wanted to work with her, and who had a rather explosive temper. Apparently he had promised his fallen comrades that he would look out for their families, and he was still taking that promise very seriously. The lady had no knowledge of any connection to the Boer War in her family. He named his comrade as a General Matthews, "a very fine officer". He had apparently made the same promise to several comrades.

After we had sat quietly for some time, he spoke through Keith. He said that he had never felt such a power as we had, nor such peace or love. It had made him realise that he needed more training. He also told us that "hundreds" of other souls, who like him had been earthbound, were being brought into the light – "from all walks of life".

In the spring of 2005 Keith's niece, Sally, who worked at a filling station just outside of Wick, had to stop using her car because one day on her way to work, she'd found herself on a different road and had not known how she had got there. Her doctor had advised her to stop driving while they investigated. Consequently she had called on her uncle for lifts home – she could get there by bus, but not home.

A couple of months later the doctors had found nothing so she decided to start driving again. On the last time that Keith had to pick her up I was with him. During our conversations on the journey home she told us that quite often things in the storeroom would be moved, and she sometimes felt presences. These never bothered her and she just dismissed them. Even one day when she was closing up and from outside had heard a great clatter of things falling. The next morning the staff had inexplicably found cans of drink all over the storeroom floor.

We told her that it sounded as if someone was seeking help, so we went there the following evening at the end of her shift to see what we could find. Keith became aware of a lady in the shop, and between us we pieced together the story. This lady, Sheila, had gathered to her many souls -many of whom were children - from around the area, which included Lansdown where the famous battle had been fought. She was trying to get help for them to move on. She had been trying for many years, but some householders had ignored her attempts to get their attention, some had moved house, and some had called in an exorcist, who was no help at all. (Exorcists tend to try to 'banish evil spirits', which upsets those who do not consider themselves to be evil – and so can make things worse, and is no help to those who do not know where to go or how to get there). She had known of Sally's connection to Keith and so was trying to get her attention without frightening her or causing harm. It was she and another lady, Joan, who had caused Sally to take a different route to work that day – one which was in fact a better route – hoping that she would stop driving for a while and therefore would have to contact Keith for help. We were only too delighted to be able to help them on their way.

Since then we periodically find other souls that have gathered there and are patiently waiting for us to go there (or to just pass by in our car whilst sending out thoughts to them) to help them cross over.

June 2006. Davey, our medium friend, rang us to ask our help. The all-female staff of the Newport shop of the national company he worked for had been aware of presences in the building – they would hear the sound of running feet upstairs when no-one was there; the electrics would go off for no reason; they would hear voices; someone saying "boo" ... The management had scoffed at these claims, so Davey had tried to help and was able to clear many souls. He did not know, however, that there was a cellar, and the disturbances had continued. One night when the shop was closed an alarm went off that brought the police round. Upon gaining entry they heard many voices upstairs so called out the riot squad. But they found no-one there! After that the management had to believe them and so asked Davey to help.

Davey felt that there had been a fire there a long time ago.

On Monday 19th June he took us to the shop at closing time, 5 p.m. The upper floors were virtually empty. On the topmost floor, where the walls had been dismantled, leaving only their bare skeleton, I sensed a grandmotherly figure and quite a lot of young girls. She was caring for these orphans, who were working for her, doing sewing and other such tasks, whilst learning enough to be able to get jobs in service afterwards. This was in the back room. The front room felt more austere, and male – where the orphan boys had been taught skills. There were no souls there, only the emanations from the past - residual energy. It felt a happy place.

One floor down, in a bare back room Keith and Davey both tuned in. A man spoke through Davey, whilst unsteadily controlling this unfamiliar body. He was puzzled as to how and why he was using another body, and what we were doing there. I explained that we had come to help. At first he did not trust us, but later realised that we really had come to help. He knew something was wrong - he did not understand why they could see the other people in the building, but could not themselves be seen. Nor did he understand why all their furniture had been taken away.

He said that all his family had passed at the same time, so I asked if there had been a fire. He was surprised I knew about that. I said I didn't know if it was just this building or all the others, too. As he said it was an extensive fire I said that we could help all his friends and neighbours as well. Eventually he agreed to call his family to him, at which point Keith became aware of Jane. The man exclaimed, surprised, "You know my daughter?" No, she'd just told him her name. Keith also named two other of his children, Emily and Peter, and then Bronwyn, his wife. It was the children who had been heard running across the floor, and Peter who had been saying "boo". The father asked wistfully, "Will my Emily finally be able to grow up?" By this time Emily was holding Keith's hand. Then he asked "What is that light I see?" I told him to focus on it and he and his family soon left with our friends in blue. (Our helpers from the higher realms, who appear dressed in blue robes).

Davey was soon controlled by another man, asking what was going on. This was a neighbour, who then asked Di, the father, why he had come back. Apparently he had come back for little Emily who had stayed with Keith, but he could confirm that they had been taken to a house that was just like theirs had been. Whereupon the neighbour called others to him and they all left with our friends in blue.

Davey later said the fire had been maybe 150 years ago.

Before we left we checked out the cellar, which Davey had not known about earlier. As I talked to the (rather jumpy) two members of staff, Keith was controlled by a man named John, who spoke through one side of his mouth, as if he'd had a stroke. He said it was Fred who had been messing with the electrics, and that he had tried to stop him. Thereupon Davey called to Fred, and both of them were helped on their way.

Later that evening, while Keith and I were dining at home, Di came with Emily to say "thank you", and to tell us he has already learned so much that he has no need now for his house. He said our friends in blue were amazingly helpful.

On Sunday October 28th 2007, around midday, we visited Dunster Castle, a National Trust property in Somerset. It was Hallowe'en Week, and there were many families with their young children dressed in Hallowe'en costumes hoping to see ghosts. Of course, ghosts don't just appear because there is a notice saying that they are there! So I think most of the children will have been disappointed, although no doubt they will have enjoyed the spurious thrills of knowing that they might meet a ghost.

We can testify to the fact that there were ghosts there! (Although, we call them spirits, as ghosts are simply residual energies, like films on the ether, that can be seen when conditions are right, and can surprise and horrify, but cannot respond any more than can actors in a film – we were not aware of any of those). We didn't exactly *see* any spirits, but we were able to feel their presence and communicate with them.

With our friend Charlie, we started in the room just beyond the 13th century gatehouse, which the notice that read 'GHOSTS' pointed to. As soon as we entered the room we could all feel the change in atmosphere, and before I could get my pen and paper out my husband Keith had already got into communication with a soul who gave his name as Jonathan Wright, the date of 1836 and his job as a wheelwright!

Charlie meanwhile had moved to the end of the room where there was a display about the castle's ghosts, which he asked me to read to him, as, being dyslexic, he finds reading difficult. As I read about the shop assistant who had seen a man dressed in green walking into the stables and - thinking it was a visitor who had not noticed the 'closed' sign - had followed him, only to find no-one there, Keith had heard someone say, "I'm Bill. That was me. I used to sweep out the stables". I continued reading about the Lady in Grey who has been seen on the staircase, whereupon Keith said that was Betty Wainwright, who had a sister called Jane.

We then returned through the room and mounted some steps below a flight of stairs that was blocked off. Here Keith became aware of a Paul who was pushed down those stairs during an argument, and died as a result of this, though not immediately. In the room beyond this Charlie was aware of someone who had been stabbed in the back, and someone else who had been trussed up on the floor. Keith was aware of someone calling for "Tommy". Further enquiry revealed that this was Jane who was looking for her love. He had been a long-time servant who had then become a soldier.

Keith was also aware of a Dennis O-oaten (he stuttered); the fact of a military presence; and the feeling that it had been so long. Keith introduced Jane to our friends in blue, and she agreed to go with them, but asked us to tell Tommy she was looking for him if we met him. Jane was a gentle, sad, woman, who by her own admission was "not too bright". In the adjacent room we did indeed find Tommy, who was looking for Jane. Although both were in spirit they had been on different levels, so had not been able to see each other. As she had not yet gone they were able to link up and go together. Tommy had been killed, but not in battle – Keith felt he may have been the one who was stabbed in the back.

As we were leaving this room we became aware that someone was trying to push us out, as we had "done enough" (said crossly). Of course, we stayed! We felt someone in authority wanted us gone – a jailer? No. Keith was aware of lots of faces on the floor, some overlapping others, indicating a long time span. After convincing this 'jailer' that we were there to help he told us his name was Philip and that he was the officer-in-charge. When asked what year it was, Keith was given the impression that it was sometime in the 13th century. Philip asked us if we knew what year it was, so we told him it was 2007, whereupon he expressed surprise that he had been there that long – he said it didn't feel that long. Having been introduced to our friends in blue, he not only agreed to go with them, taking all his charges, but also volunteered to go around and find and help others. He said he would "be glad to get out of here". We got the impression of a very good, conscientious, reliable officer, who cared about his men.

We then moved on into the castle itself, where Keith stopped on the first turn of the Grand Staircase. He felt the strong energy of a lady dressed in a flowing blue gown, with white across the edge of the sleeves and around the neck, who would walk down the stairs and stop at that landing, looking down. I would surmise that she was either the first lady of the castle, or considered herself the belle of the ball. As people passed us on the stairs Keith felt a strong pull on his heart area. He also felt the name of 'Jane' being called, (a different Jane to the previous one). This lady, too, was helped on her way by our friends in blue.

Proceeding to the first bedroom, which had a four poster bed in it, Keith was aware of someone called Henry who suffered from migraines.

Unfortunately, time was running out for us as we had to be at the lovely Alcombe Christian Spiritualist Church for Keith to take their 3pm service, so we had to cut short our visit soon after this - but we intend to return.

We have returned twice since then, and the last time (March 2010) Keith felt that there was no-one left who needed our help.

June 2009. Our friend Harry brought a man to our Healing Clinic, not for healing, but for us to help him with presences in his flat. He had been living there for nine years and had always been aware of spirits and energies, which had been making him more and more depressed. Keith instantly tuned in and 'felt' that the problem was on the fourth floor of the block of flats, which it turned out is where he lived. I felt that although this man's problems may have been on the fourth floor, the problem was much more widespread, beyond the whole building even.

Two days later we all met at his flat off Redcliffe Hill. Keith immediately set to work and cleared many lost souls, including a father and two children who had been killed when the area was blitzed in the Second World War.

When we entered we could all feel the heaviness of the atmosphere, but as we progressed, and with Neil H's *The Resonation of Angels* CD playing, the atmosphere gradually became lighter and lighter, moving from a feeling of relief, through joy, to gratitude.

As Keith was working within the flat, I was extending my reach outside. I sensed the problems went right back to medieval times, and maybe beyond that, and right up to modern times.

The area is close to the river and would have been a settlement for many centuries, but would have been outside what I might call the 'respectable' areas of Bristol, so would in the past have been a haunt of criminals, pirates, smugglers, prostitutes and the like. It also has two graveyards nearby, and a long-established hospital. Harry's friend confirmed that he had indeed been aware of a medieval monk, as well as Victorian spirits.

We explained that this flat was only the focus of activity because of the sensitivity of the current occupant, and many of these souls were drawn here either seeking help, or for the safety they felt here. Many other souls, especially children, would have found such sanctuary in nearby homes where the occupants might very well be unaware of their presence.

By the time we left, two and a half hours later, our Kingswood Army was helping a steady stream of lost souls into the light, after which the angels would try to clear the negative energies from the whole area, (not an easy task as so many of the current inhabitants are enmeshed in negativity).

At another house-clearing recently, we were called back the following week. Although it had improved, the lady occupant felt someone was still there. As we approached the house Keith was aware that above the roof – the highest point for miles around – there was a huge shining cross. It transpired that a man called John (who appeared to be an old neighbour from across the road) had refused to go the last time we were there as he had promised to wait for someone, and had now found him so wanted us back so they could both go. It also transpired that the shining cross above the house was in fact Archangel Jophiel, who oversees our Healing Clinic.

A more recent incident of a long-dead soul not realising they were dead, and so still feeling pain, was related to me by a fellow student at a Crystal Healing course we were both on.

She had been to a workshop on 'Healing your Ancestors' and had been asked to write the names of all ancestors that she had known on a sheet of paper and then, holding her hands on it, pray for them to be healed of any and all things that still troubled them. She had become aware of her grandfather who had died when she was just four years old – many decades earlier. He commented to her on the pain he still felt. Later he had come to her again, free at last from pain, and very grateful!

Apparently you can do this for others too, even if you never knew them. As a topical example the whole group had done it for Barak Obama's ancestors,. It would seem that this is an important work that would benefit from many people doing it in the privacy of their own homes – however, make sure you do it from a centre of spirituality, and ask for help and protection from those from the Higher Realms – God, Jesus, Saints, Masters, angels ... And always for their highest good.

Just recently we were asked to try to help someone the other side of the country whose parents were having problems of a paranormal nature in their home. Being too far to travel we were provided with a set of photos of the house and the two rooms affected, one above the other.

On first tuning in I felt that the 1930s house had been built on land that had previously had part of another building on it. I felt that a part of this bungalow had been build on open land that had been used many years ago to bury those poor souls that had died of 'pestilence', i.e. the Black Death. Some at least of the feelings that the current occupants were sensing was the residual energy from those times. Keith and I also sensed more recent souls there in need of help, so we asked our friends in blue to go take a look and sort it out.

In view of all these experiences and many more, I have come to the conclusion that there are a lot more souls 'stuck' than we were led to believe. In Spiritualism we were taught that everyone is met at death and led away to where-ever they are meant to go.

It seems to me, though, that many remain stuck having refused to go anywhere with such souls for various reasons. Some don't go because, believing that there is nothing after death, they do not accept they are dead, it being patently obvious to them that they are not. Many have not even noticed the change. Others stay because they have unfinished business; a place or a person they don't wish to leave; or just because they are happy where they are. Many have been indoctrinated with the notion that there are only two or three choices, heaven or hell or maybe purgatory, the latter two being very unpleasant places, and so, not believing they are good enough to go to heaven, prefer to stay where they are, thank you very much.

One who was very happy where they were was the most helpful spirit I have ever heard of.

My new friend B says that in the house where her family lived for a while, if you left dirty dishes out in the evening, by the morning they would be washed up and put away. When you brought in a basketful of laundry from the line and went out to get the second load in, the first lot would be neatly folded; and after you took them upstairs and put them away the second load would also be neatly folded. The soul responsible had served several families at this address this way.

I want one like that! Who wouldn't?

Apparently not the next people to move into that house – they called in a priest to get rid of her! Not a good idea, as after she left, knowing when she was not wanted, other spirits that she had obviously been keeping under control, ran riot. Within a short space of time they had been flooded twice, and their house was burnt down.

A former colleague suffered a sudden heart attack and died just before we left for our annual fortnight's holiday. We found out about it when we returned, by which time he'd had his funeral. It was a bit of a shock as he was not yet 50.

Washing-up at the kitchen sink the next day, and thinking about him, I became aware of him standing behind me. I telepathically said "Hello". There was a pregnant pause, and then he said, almost accusingly, "You're talking to me! No-one's talking to me any more."

Realising what that meant I said that was because, unlike me, most people couldn't see him, because he was what the world calls 'dead'.

Immediately he responded indignantly, "I can't be dead. I've got too much to do!"

I told him I was sorry about that, but there was nothing either he or I could do about it – he'd even had his funeral.

It seems he had been wandering about the homes of friends and family, puzzling as to why everyone was ignoring him.

I told him of the wonderful colours I understood were in the next world - colours such as are never seen on earth, suggesting that, as a lover of art, he would really appreciate them.

He came back a few days later to say 'thank you'. He had quickly adjusted to his new situation.

When I spoke of this to another colleague, who knew him better than I did, she said that was just like him – if Plan A didn't work, he would scrap it and go straight on to Plan B.

A few weeks later we were attending a Spiritualist Church service where the medium was an old friend of ours, Sam McDowell. He came to me and gave me a name I took to be a first name, as is usually the case, and which I did not recognise. Keith nudged me and reminded me of this colleague – it was his surname! That was the extent of the message – he had typically just popped in to try his hand at this. I haven't heard from him since.

Hallowe'en Ghostwatch
October 31st – November 1st 2004

Craig-y-Nos Castle

Along with 78 other people, Keith and I attended this Hallowe'en Ghostwatch organised by Bill Harrison and Patrick Gamble. The previous evening there had been 108 people, all rushing around trying to see ghosts, or get orbs on cameras or sounds on tapes.

Craig-y-Nos is a neo-gothic castle built in 1843 on the banks of the River Tawe in the Brecon Beacons which was owned and lived in from 1878 to 1919 by a famous and talented opera diva, Madame Adelina Patti, who had moved in the highest echelons of Victorian society, including entertaining European royalty. She had built a complete theatre there which could hold 150 people. Later the castle was used as a chest hospital from 1922 to 1959, which included tuberculosis sufferers, and had additional buildings erected for the nurses to stay in, which is where we stayed – not that we slept much!

Soon after we arrived we walked around the outside before it got dark. At the back, on a path by some railings, above the steps leading to a statue of a white hart, Keith became aware of a young girl outside by the porch. She was about three feet tall, with fair hair, dressed in a white pinafore over a black dress, and with a slight problem with her neck.

He later re-connected with this young girl in the Blue Bar, which opens onto the same path. She said her name was Martha, she was 10 years old, and had come from Bristol when she was ill with tuberculosis. She said this was when she was four, but when I expressed surprise at this she amended it to seven. This made me suspect she was telling us what she thought would please us - or the first thing that came into her head – not necessarily the truth. *[I found out later that other people had also 'picked up' a young girl called Martha]*. She said she was alone; played around downstairs; likes people and shows herself sometimes. She also said there are four spirit children that she plays with. Keith felt her give him a hug and a kiss on the cheek. I asked her permission to take her photo, which she gave gladly, and sat on the chair next to Keith – but it did not show anything unusual. (*I later took a photo of the back porch, and some have said they can see in it a monk, an angel, and the girl. I can see the girl if I look at the picture as if it were a 'magic eye' picture - she appears as a hazy outline looking over the railings – see page 43*).

Soon after 9 p.m. I went to Madame Patti's bedroom, where I sat alone in the dark, admiring the view over the trees with the mountains behind, all bathed in the light of a full moon. (*Most other people were at the clairvoyant demonstration; I was struggling against the effects of a migraine, from someone's thoughtless action with some perfume at a fayre the previous day*). Later people were coming and going, but I sat there for an hour and a half, during which time two women also sat quietly. They had arrived with Bill's group, but stayed on after the rest left. (*Before Bill's group arrived there was a group from the radio company recording their resident medium. Keith was aware of a Native American with one of the women in their team, and told her so, saying he felt he was called Red Feather, and was from the Lakota Sioux tribe*).

As we were sitting quietly in this room, many times we were interrupted by others on this Ghostwatch who would open the door, shine their torches around the room – level with our eyes – and say something like "there's nothing here, let's try somewhere else". As if 'ghosts' would just be hanging around waiting to be seen! Or would show up by torch-light!

During a quiet spell I became aware of a girl of about six years old with flaxen ringlets and wearing a fancy cherry-red dress, in the style of a ball gown, but shorter. I got the impression that the dress had been made from some satin-like cloth from a lady's dress. The girl was very proud of her dress. (*The following day in the dining room, I saw a portrait of Madame Patti wearing a dress the same colour*). We were then interrupted, and following their departure, I felt the girl was a spoilt child and peeved at being ignored, so I asked her permission to take her photo, which was readily granted and seemed to improve her mood.

This photo shows an orb where I felt the girl was standing, at about her head height, but nothing else unusual.

11.30 p.m. On the way to the cellars we went behind the stage, but felt nothing. The four of us later settled in an alcove in the cellar in the pitch black – in a circle on four chairs, holding hands to try to build up some energy. I became aware of a young man called Peter who telepathically told me that he had worked on the grounds, and then another, shorter, young man by the name of David joined Peter. They were both aged about 14. At the start of the First World War the older groundsmen had joined up, leaving the two younger ones with far too great a responsibility. At that point the older lady 'saw' the grounds flooded.

Shortly after this someone tried to 'build' in the centre of us, but gave up as the energy was too low. He then spoke through Keith instead. He said his name was John and that he and the others were fed up with all these people trying to contact them, get them to make orbs, noises etc. He came to us four as we were prepared to sit quietly and wait. He then discovered that, through Keith and me, he could be freed from this place – Peter and David decided to go too, and some of the others. John told us he had come to the house in 1922 when his mother had left him there as a young child because he was ill. His health had recovered each summer and deteriorated each winter. He thought he had passed in 1932.

Keith took two photos here on a digital camera – the first showed only our knees and feet, but the second also showed a large bright bone-shaped light to the left of Keith. (In a pitch black cellar, remember).

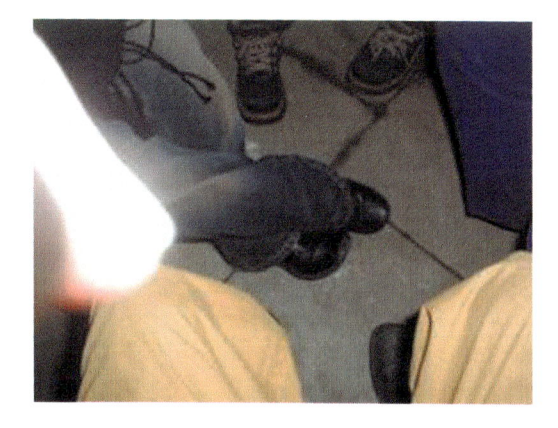

Keith and I had been invited to appear live on 'The Wave', a radio programme on Swansea Sound. This was being done on the stage of the theatre. Chris (the presenter) asked Keith to try to channel someone. After a little while 'tuning in', Keith was spoken through by a man who had difficulty speaking, as he'd had a bad throat at the end of his life. In response to my questioning, he said his name was Tom, and that he had first come to the castle in the 1880s, as a lad of about 12, straight from school, to work on the grounds. He had lived just down the road. He said that Madame Patti was "a very very kind person". He told us he'd eventually become the Head Gardener. The radio crew were "astounded", they'd never seen anything like it! Paul (an assistant presenter) said that they would put the interview onto their web-site. Chris wanted to try again later, which we did, but the energy was too low by then (it was 1.30 a.m. and people were getting tired), although a Bill tried.

Soon after the show finished all the radio crew left except Paul, who was fascinated by it all. Some of the crew earlier had tried to hold a "séance" in one of the rooms upstairs but had felt that they had been told in no uncertain terms to "get out". He asked us if we would go back with him and find out more, so the five of us, (including the two ladies – the younger one having also been live on air with us), went upstairs, only to find that room occupied, so we went next door.

We stood in a circle linking hands and eventually Bill spoke through Keith. He said he would not answer questions – he had come as he'd heard that through us he could be freed. He also was tired of all the demands and wanted his freedom. He said he would come back when he was needed, as would the others, because they all appreciated that it helped the owner to restore "this beautiful building", but they would no longer be trapped there.

Paul had taken a lot of photos which had orbs on, he'd also felt something he'd never felt before. He'd come expecting to laugh, but was now fascinated. Keith and I spent another one and half hours talking to him by the log fire. He left at gone four a.m. – a convert. Then we went to bed.

Keith had five photos with orbs on. Helen's photos taken on a traditional camera showed none, but people have said they can see various figures in the shot below - outside at the rear of the building, as mentioned earlier.

These two photos may also interest you. They were sent to me some years ago by a very dear friend.

The first shows the celebration of a birthday, with lots of orbs. The second shows orbs that have patterns inside them. My friend assures me that no-one had been blowing bubbles, and no-one saw these orbs at the time.

The above photo was taken more recently by a new acquaintance, Gary, in his lounge. Many of these also have patterns in them.

You may also be interested in the following photos taken during the August 1999 eclipse of the sun from a camp site in Cornwall, which was the only county in the UK from where the full eclipse could be seen. It was a new and very basic campsite, with no lights and very few facilities, not even hot water, and with compost toilets, but it was all our Vegan Camp organisers could get, as everywhere else was fully booked. It was situated in a valley and amongst fields, inland from the coastal town of Falmouth.

It was the photographer's first visit to Vegan Camp as he had come especially for the eclipse, but as a vegan he was delighted to be able to stay with us. He had set up his equipment on the higher, south, side of the valley, as had others. We had opted to watch the eclipse from the north side of the valley, which was where we were all camped. The eclipse was due at noon on this cloudy day.

As luck would have it, those on the south side of the valley couldn't see the eclipse for the clouds, but we saw it through a small break in the clouds at just the right moment – rather like looking through a small oblong window, or a television screen. Keith was amazed at the power he felt from it! It was fantastic – we didn't even need special glasses as there was just enough cloud to do the job. We saw it all!

Our disappointed new friend, Dave Hope, looked across at us and was dumbfounded to see beyond us several coloured lights moving about above an otherwise empty field, and so he took this photo. He said they were white, orange and red, and moving quite fast when not hovering. It's not a very clear photo, but you can see that there are lights in the sky that were obviously moving.

Moving lights in the air during the Aug 1999 eclipse

I have also included this similar view for comparison.

Furthermore, when he got home and viewed the video that had been left running on auto on a tripod, he was surprised to see that at the height of the eclipse there were pin-pricks of white light moving in the sky in a very odd manner.

When the sky began to lighten, he also saw, on the video, what he described as "like some sort of cloaking device" (á la Star Trek) which appeared in the centre of the screen and moved across to the right and out of shot.

He says it should be remembered that the lights in the photos and on the video may be attributed to natural phenomenon e.g. ball lightning. This would not make it any less paranormal given that paranormal means "beyond the scope of normal objective ... explanation" as the Oxford Compact English Dictionary puts it.

The next day he made a thorough investigation all round that area to try to ascertain where the lights had come from – but could find nothing to explain them!

Fighting the Good Fight

Of course, not all spirits feel in need of help crossing over, sometimes they enjoy making mischief - or worse.

When I was working in Bristol's Central Library one of my young colleagues was a lovely girl – bright as a button, interested in all sorts of things and very willing. This changed after she played with 'the glass'. She was absent for three months, being treated in Barrow Gurney, the old mental asylum, for mental problems. When she finally came back to work she just was not the same. Occasionally you could see the old her, but more often than not she had a far-away look in her eyes, and just did not seem to be 'with it'.

Being new to Spiritualism at the time I did not know how to help.

Since then I have known another young person who went with some friends to a cemetery at night, armed with candles, in an attempt to contact the dead. What madness! He told me they had indeed contacted someone – a violent criminal. His friends were so frightened that they never went back, but he told me that he intended to. I tried my best to talk him out of it, but it seems that he went, because the next I heard he was in trouble with the police for a violent crime he swears he never committed, but where all the evidence, some of which he gave the police himself, pointed to him.

What people fail to realise is that spirits are just people, with all the usual faults and failings. So if you want to contact them and do not make it perfectly clear that you only want good spirits, then you are more than likely to get the bad ones who, having more power than you (i.e. more knowledge, as knowledge is power) will have mischievous or even malicious fun at your expense, leaving you to bear the blame. It's not the fault of the glass, or the ouija board it's just the way they are used.

We met Mrs M. when we were involved with Grosvenor Road Church. She had sat in a development circle for forty years without developing any psychic gift – she was their 'power-house'. She was, however, able to use a ouija board. Every time before she used it she would say a prayer for protection and the Lord's Prayer, and every time afterwards she would say a prayer of thanks. She really did use it religiously and with proper respect, and so she never attracted any lower spirits. She actually passed it on to us towards the end of her life, as she did not want it to fall into the wrong hands. We still have it somewhere, although we have never used it – it is too primitive a way of communication for us. It is not the ouija board or the glass, which is dangerous but the manner in which they are used. Too often they are used frivolously, sometimes with dire consequences.

A few years ago we were called to a house in Frampton Cottrell where the teenage daughter had been having fits for the past six months. The parents had only just found out that these had started after she had joined her brother, sister and some friends when they used a ouija board that they had made themselves.

Firstly we helped some souls there cross over. On a subsequent visit we persuaded some that had been attracted by the activity to move on. Each time we visited we gave the daughter healing – which did help some but did not entirely resolve the problem. On a final visit Keith was upstairs when he was told by Archangel Michael that when he gave healing downstairs Archangel Raphael would be with him. And so it was. A stubborn possessing soul suddenly came out of the girl, entered Keith and was immediately taken away by Raphael. This finally returned the girl to her former health, though rather chastened by the experience – as were her siblings.

Sometimes these cases are like peeling an onion, layer by layer. One has to deal with the easier outer layers which serve to obscure the real problem before gradually getting down to the core of the matter.

Another case we know of is when a curious young man experimenting with a ouija board in his own room unwittingly let loose the hordes of Hell on his neighbour. Only her staunch faith and strong character saw her through the next few years, whilst Keith and I and a mutual friend strove hard to rid her and the surrounding area of these souls of the Darkness. We brought many of them into the Light, but there were always more to take their places. In so doing we all experienced a sharp learning curve! Early on we learnt that she lived in an area well known for the amount of black magic that is still practised.

This was in the late 1990s and on a visit to her home Keith felt that just beyond the end of the row of terraced houses there had been a witch's coven which had been operational for 400 years. This was later confirmed by a local resident who showed us an entry in a book to that effect.

As part of our efforts to help her we had sat with our friend Davey in his home outside of Bath. As we opened up and called on the Light and our helpers from the higher realms, Keith saw in the centre of the three of us a very short slim man with a beard, dressed in a tight-fitting black garment with the hood up around his face. He was looking around in surprise and bemusement. It seems he had been just passing through minding his own business when he had suddenly felt himself caught in our energies - energies such as he had never felt before, and found he liked. After observing what we were doing, and following some discussion later, he decided to join us and has helped us many times since.

In the same circumstances, at a different time, I was acting as intermediary between a spirit helper who was talking through Keith, and an evil spirit that was talking through Davey. We had called on Archangel Michael with his sword Excalibur to help us. Suddenly Davey's face was thrust close up to mine as the entity said, very menacingly, "I will eat your soul". I just laughed and said, "Think how much Light you will have inside you then!" Taken aback because I had not been scared, and also having to consider what it would be like if I was right, he hesitated, and with that Archangel Michael came in with his sword and took him away.

Another time when we were at our home, Keith was on the phone to our friend trying to persuade a dark spirit to leave her alone - with little success. But then this spirit took the offensive and came close to Keith in order to defeat him. Instead he found himself in energies he had not felt before and did not recognise, but which he also found he liked. As Keith told him, the energy was simply love, pure love. Keith was able to re-unite him with his lost loved ones from long ago and he went with them to the Light. After some re-adjustment and training he came back to help us, knowing that by his former comrades-in-arms he would be called 'traitor', and he has helped rescue souls from the dark many times since.

I hope I have said enough to ensure that any readers will think long and hard before attempting to contact spirit, and will then, if they decide to proceed, do so only with pure, unselfish motives and extreme caution, in a humble and loving manner.

It is also most important that no-one tries to do this sort of work unless they are totally free of fear - and have sufficient back-up in the form of competent mediums and spirit helpers from the higher realms.

We are, in fact, only the front runners of a huge team without whose help we would not be able to do what we do. Many souls who have been surviving in darkness without ever knowing love have been persuaded to go to the Light and are so grateful that they make themselves available to help us whenever we need them – we call them our 'Kingswood Army' because it was from our work in Kingswood that we first found many souls wanting to repay our kindness in this way. They work under the direction and alongside our 'friends in blue' who are beautiful souls working under the guidance of Archangel Michael. Our friends in blue, both male and female, often work in threes, so we also call them, light-heartedly, Tom, Dick and Harry! They don't mind, they sometimes refer to themselves as that now. They have quite a sense of fun.

Animal Tales

Young robin

Many years ago I heard tell of an Anglican Church where, during the service, a bird gained entry somehow and was causing a disturbance flying around trying to find a way out again – so much so that eventually someone killed it, so that they could carry on with the service undisturbed.

A short time later I heard of a similar incident in the church at Stansted (a Spiritualist College) which was handled very differently – the congregation were asked to all concentrate their thoughts on the little sparrow and direct it to escape through an open window. After a short time the bird happily flew out and away! I mention this to highlight the very different attitudes to God's little creatures, and what can be done when people combine to use the power of thought.

Some years after we had moved into our house our next-door neighbour acquired a lovely dog that we made friends with. Years later they had moved out but we would see the dog in the local shop which her owners ran. By that time (1983) the dog was suffering from old age and she would manoeuvre herself until one of my hands was petting her head and the other was giving healing to her haunches. We would stay like that, in the middle of the shop, for maybe 10-15 minutes then she would move away as if she knew that was enough healing for one day. Her owner said she never stayed that still for anyone else, and if she hadn't seen it for herself she would never have believed it.

Descent from Pecca Falls, 2001

On New Year's Eve 2001, we were spending a few days with friends at a vegan B & B in the Lake District, near Kendal. The landscape was lightly dusted with snow which several sunny days had failed to melt. Keith and I took advantage of the beautiful sunshine to go for a walk along the Ingleton Falls in West Yorkshire. Of the 4½ mile circular walk only the first mile was open as beyond that we were told it was too treacherous.

We must have been the last to arrive as everyone else was in front of us - and it was busy. We carefully wended our way to the foot of the series of waterfalls that makes up Pecca Falls, and Keith decided to go no further. After talking to people coming back down from the top of the falls I decided to ascend – very carefully. It was well worth it, the falls were spectacular! On the way back down, as pictured above, I slipped and sat down rather abruptly, but picked myself up unharmed and carried on even more carefully. Keith and I then cautiously picked our way back along the valley as the sun began to set.

Having reached the wide and level path at the bottom my guard must have dropped a bit as suddenly I found myself flat on my back, screaming with pain. I felt the back of my fingers being gently pinched and told Keith that I could feel that, but he told me it wasn't him - a robin had flown down and slowly hopped nearer. It was the robin, not Keith, who had touched my fingers. As Keith gently talked to him, I raised my head to take a look. He was right by my side looking concerned. After a while my back was beginning to get cold so I asked Keith to help me up. The robin hopped away a little until I was on my feet again, and then hopped back. He stood there at our feet, looking up at us. We had nothing to give him so we blew him some kisses and as we left he flew up into a tree, then down to the river. I could have done without the broken wrist, but the memory of that close encounter, far from home, with a little robin redbreast will stay with us both for a very long time.

One call-out in 2002 gave us a magical experience with some race horses. We were asked to visit a stud farm in Dorset where there had been a series of problems involving the horses. The lady had taken over a farm 17 years previously, with her husband, and had then fought to be allowed to breed racehorses rather than use the land for agricultural purposes. She had bred some lovely animals but had recently come to realise that the foals she sold did well, but any she tried to race herself had unusual things happen to them. One had damaged a rear leg with its own front hoof, and would have been 'put down' if they had not objected. Another had been all ready to race when the race had been cancelled. The jockey had taken the saddle off and put the horse back in the stable, instead of running it as he should have done, to get rid of its pent-up energy. It died of a heart attack.

She had been given our name and asked us if we could find out what was happening and why, and do something about it.

We began by having a tour of the property with the lady and her sister-in-law. In a rather large field there were a dozen or so of these beautiful horses, aged between one and four years. I have ridden horses a few times over the years, but I wouldn't say I was particularly au fait with them and I held back a little, as did Keith. As the two ladies wandered back, chatting away, I turned to follow, but found my way blocked by some of these horses. I turned to go another way, but discovered that both Keith and I were surrounded by all the horses! One of them was licking at my jacket – I assumed they wanted apples or sugar cubes or something, but we had nothing. I knew they meant no harm so I wasn't frightened, but I didn't know what to do – I didn't want to spook them - so I said rather loudly "Gosh, we're surrounded!" When the lady realised what was happening she came back and shooed them away. She was amazed, as they usually avoid strangers – and they never get fed in the field! They were the most beautiful creatures and I felt privileged to be so treated by them – I will treasure the memory of that magic moment. We felt quite honoured.

The stables that the horses used had been converted from an old battery chicken shed, as had another shed which was used to house the tackle. Not unexpectedly we had found the atmosphere in and around the two sheds to be very heavy. Keith had tuned in and brought a great deal of Light to bear on them, not stopping until he felt satisfied that the desired result had been obtained.

A few days later the lady rang to tell us that she could feel the difference.

Rhia with Mairi 2007

In January 2007, while Keith was giving his usual healing to Mairi in her home, I tried to communicate with her rescued greyhound, Rhia. Mairi was concerned that Rhia should know that she was safe with her, and asked if I could try to help. I didn't know if I could, but I was willing to try.

Apparently, Rhia had raced for more than four years before being adopted by a greyhound rescue organisation that had homed her with a man with whom she had stayed for three years. But the man had had a heart attack and poor Rhia had been alone with his body for over 12 hours before anyone came. Mairi suffered with her back, occasionally being laid up in bed with it, and suspected that Rhia had been unsettled by this.

I had never before attempted to read the thoughts and feelings of any animal but I gave it a go. I felt that Rhia was indeed unsettled by this, as she was concerned that the same thing would happen to Mairi as had happened to her previous guardian, and so she felt insecure and worried.

Mairi asked me to tell Rhia that the man had had a pre-existing heart problem, which was life-threatening, unlike the problem she, Mairi, suffered with. Also she wanted me to tell her that she loved Rhia very much, and that she would have a home with her for the rest of her life. Putting that into images, not words, was difficult, but I did my best and felt Rhia at least understood the last part, and returned that love.

The following week Mairi told us that Rhia had been much calmer since then and seemed more secure. She then asked me to see if I could help Rhia overcome her fear of, and aggression towards, other dogs, especially terriers. Again I tried to mentally convey that to Rhia, who this time seemed eager for me to communicate with her, and even disappointed that I didn't do so as soon as we got there. The previous week Mairi had also wanted to know if Rhia would like her to adopt another greyhound as a companion. I felt that Rhia was tempted, but didn't want to share the love she received from Mairi.

The next week Mairi wanted me to see what I could find out about Rhia's former life, starting with her parents. I felt that Rhia did not know who her father was, but had been loved by her mother, who was of a smaller stature to the adult Rhia and her brothers, but sturdy. She had also had sisters but they had disappeared from her life early on, whereas two of her brothers had been with Rhia in the same racing stables for quite some time, before first one and then the other disappeared. They had seen their mother from time to time, and she had borne at least two other litters, until she too, disappeared. She had also seen an injured greyhound shot, which had traumatised her; Mairi later told me that Rhia is really terrified of the sound of fireworks. However Rhia had enjoyed racing, and all the attention she got both before and after the races, especially when she won. Apart from her brothers she had never bonded with any other dogs – and the only ones she had seen were other greyhounds and the occasional small dog or Alsatian. I tried to convey the feeling to her that the other dogs – and indeed cats – that she met on her walks were no threat to her and must not be barked at or chased. Since then, Mairi says that Rhia has been very much better behaved when out walking.

It seemed that since the previous week Rhia had considered the question of a companion animal for her and now wanted a puppy (not necessarily a greyhound) that she could mother, and who would then grow into a companion for her. It felt to me like a small girl wanting to play mother with a real baby, because she wanted someone all her own to love. I told her (I hope) that that was asking a lot, and it would depend on how well she could learn to behave with other dogs, especially the smaller ones. I didn't tell Mairi this bit, but decided to wait a week and see if Rhia's behaviour changed.

Later I checked with her and it seemed that she had changed her mind, after I had told her that puppies grow up quickly, and would in any case be competition for Mairi's attention and affections.

I also had a 'word' with her about her habit of weeing on the carpet, especially at night, and have told her to ask to be let out. Also I have asked her to alert Mairi if there is anyone at the door, as her hearing is sharper than Mairi's. Since then I have heard her yelp to ask to have the door opened – I had never heard her make a sound before. She now very seldom has 'accidents' on the carpet, and always waits or asks to be let out.

Mairi had bought a woven dog basket for her, but Rhia didn't use it, so I was asked to find out Rhia's thoughts on this. It appeared it was too small for Rhia, who liked to stretch out, but also it was too hard – having not much fur and very little fat it was uncomfortable for her. So Mairi changed it for a soft pillow and blanket, which Rhia seems to be quite happy with.

On another occasion Rhia seemed especially excited when we arrived, and hardly able to contain herself. However, she had to wait until Keith gave Mairi healing. When I invited her to communicate with me it appeared she had realised that she could ask me for something – she wanted to have a large bone! Mairi always used to give her dogs bones, but the last one had not been interested in them, so she had forgotten all about them. On being reminded she speedily bought one, which Rhia has subsequently gnawed on for several hours every day. The next time Rhia saw me she made a point of thanking me for this.

All in all, Mairi is extremely pleased with the result, Rhia seems much calmer and happier (she even has a Rottweiler 'boyfriend' now) and I have a new string to my bow.

Our vegan friend Dave Hope - who took the photos of the 1999 eclipse - told me the following about his deaf Dalmatian dog Dorothy - his picture of her appears below.

Aged about 14 years, she developed cancer which manifested as large lumps under her skin. She had two under her belly that eventually looked like two red tomatoes, and several on other parts of her body. Her hair had fallen out and her skin was patchily red. She was suffering so much that Dave rang the veterinary practice one Saturday evening and it was arranged that a vet would visit Sunday morning to put her out of her misery. That night Dave stayed up with Dorothy all night, watching television from the sofa, with the dog's head resting on his lap. Late into the evening Dave was flipping through the channels when he chanced upon the God channel – one of those evangelistic American ones. He is a Quaker and so does not like this style and never watches it. However, he heard a woman on there saying that if you have a pet suffering from cancer this is what you must do… Naturally he listened and then followed the advice. After saying the Lord's Prayer over his dog he repeated several times what he had been told to say– "there's no pain in Heaven so there is no pain on Earth" - this accords with the sentence of the Lord's Prayer "on Earth as it is in Heaven". He then fell asleep on the floor, with Dorothy sleeping above him on the sofa. He was awoken hours later when Dorothy woke up and fell off the sofa onto him. The two 'red tomatoes' had gone, and the others elsewhere had decreased in size! He didn't know what to do about the visit from the vet, but after discussing it with a friend he decided to let it stand – but the vet did not come. The next morning (Monday) Dorothy was again improved, and the remaining lumps were visibly decreasing in size, almost as you watched. When he rang the vet's practice, saying about how the vet had not come on the Sunday morning he was told that vets never do that on a Sunday, and they didn't know why he had been told that. When he took Dorothy to see the vet – now having no lumps and her hair having grown back – the vet couldn't believe it. She said that she had never seen such a thing and that it was impossible for a dog to get better so quickly without chemotherapy! Dave was delighted and took Dorothy out for many walks, which she loved. They had 12 more weeks together. The last week of her life the lumps came back, and this time the prayers didn't work, but they progressed quickly so she didn't suffer much. She was 14½ years old – a good age for a deaf Dalmatian – and we all have to go sometime, but Dave was so pleased to have the healthy Dorothy back for a few more months before she passed.

Another tale he told me concerned his father and a guinea-pig. His father was in a care home many miles away suffering from dementia. Dave keeps guinea-pigs and runs a guinea-pig sanctuary. At that time he had a litter of six guinea-pigs and their mother. The youngsters were less than a year old. One of them, Mandy, was very pretty with a lovely nature and Dave would take her with him when he visited his father. His Dad would hold Mandy on his lap, stroking her. He called her his puppy, and was very fond of her. In August 2010 at 10.15 in the morning his Dad passed on, and Dave was very upset. He'd seen to the guinea-pigs about 8 o'clock that morning and they were all there, happy and healthy. He didn't revisit them until the evening and counting them in he couldn't see Mandy. He rattled the nuggets in the tin – no Mandy came running. He looked in the outside run – no Mandy. He picked up the little house – and there was Mandy, dead. The time was 10.15 in the evening. She had obviously been dead for some time, but the day before he had taken pictures of them all, all healthy. It could have been a bizarre coincidence, but I feel that Mandy had formed a bond with Dave's Dad and so had opted to accompany him into the next world.

Animals frequently figure in people's experiences of the paranormal within their own homes, but seldom are people distressed by this, usually recognising their own pets.

At one of my meditation groups early in 2008 spirit commented on the many pets who, when they 'die' remain with their human friends.

Sometimes, when their human friend passes on, it is this animal friend who calls for help for them if they get stuck and need help to cross over.

Apparently there are small groups of ex-pets who choose to remain near the earth in order to help souls who are 'lost', but who don't trust people. They, like their human counterparts, enjoy a rest, in between this work, in homes that are filled with love - but only with the consent of the rightful inhabitants.

These next tales are not about any animal, but neither do they fit into any other chapter, so I'll tell them here.

A very spiritual and sensitive friend of ours was in the kitchen at the back of her house when she heard a scream coming from outside the front of her house, which faced fields and hedges. She rushed into her front room and saw a big old tree opposite being bulldozed to make way for the Longwell Green mini-town. It was the tree that she could hear screaming.

A bit later we spent a week in a caravan with our two children in the Brecon Beacons above Abergavenny. One very windy day I was reading a book to my children when I became aware that the stand of trees a hundred yards down the hill from us were feeling very uneasy. Tuning in more, I sensed they were afraid of burning. I could see no reason for this, so I sent out thoughts to them to calm them down. The next day we heard there had been a very extensive forest fire in France. Was the smell carried on the wind? Somehow those trees knew of the danger, although obviously not how remote it was.

One Bonfire Night at home, I was at the kitchen sink watching Keith and the children enjoying a big bonfire, when I felt the terror from the neighbouring pine trees. I assured them they were in no danger, and they calmed down, although not liking it. However, the next morning the ones nearest the fire had many scorched branches, much to our chagrin.

Another incident involving plants occurred many years ago. I was upset with a close friend of mine, who had seemed to be ignoring me. He must have realised something was wrong, as one day he brought me in a bunch of white chrysanthemums from his garden. This did not please me however, and I was furious that he thought that would make everything right. I angrily threw the flowers into the bin. However, as I did so I felt the spirit of the flowers break – they had been given with love and were heart-broken to have been rejected so angrily! (I know they don't actually have hearts, but that's the closest I can get to describing what I felt).

Finally, a more recent experience involving living creatures, although not what most people would think of as 'animals'.

My disabled friend Bez had been living for several years in a flat that had been condemned 10 years previously – long before she had been put into it. It was recently re-condemned, and she has now been moved into a new home.

When the weather was damp, so was her ground-floor flat! On top of which in the colder months her first job every morning was to evict the numerous overnight squatters – slugs, snails, worms, spiders, earwigs, woodlice, centipedes and silver fish.

Meanwhile in the October 2010 issue of Beryl Sevior's 'Echoes' I read a channelling from Archangel Michael concerning our unused potential which included the following: - "Maybe you could also create an energy matting to cover the areas where there has been flooding so that the dirt will not swirl into these places causing more chaos for them to meet with. You could visualize all the buildings in whatever form they may be being reinforced with energy walls, floors and roofs, making them more secure." Wow! Really? Our thoughts could keep the dirt out?!

Then it occurred to me that if it could work with dirt then surely it could also work with living creatures, so I experimented by visualizing an energy matting all around the inside of Bez's flat with the intention of keeping the creepy-crawlies out. I didn't tell her about this until she told me that the slugs and snails were no longer coming in. The others were though, so I tried visualizing stronger, thicker, denser matting. It worked! Bez topped it up herself from time to time, but there had been no more creepy-crawlies in the flat since – despite the cold, wet, weather.

Another tool to add to our belts!

If you would like to subscribe to the bi-monthly 'Echoes' – the Echoes of the Masters and our Hearts as channelled by Beryl Sevior, a BDAH member(Bristol District Association of Healers) – then contact her at 2 Kent Way, North Worle, Weston super Mare, Somerset BS22 7QR.

Clairvoyance

Me in 2000

I do not remember many of the messages I give, because as I tune in to spirit and strive to relay what I am getting clairsentiently as accurately as I can, my memory seems to go to sleep. This is probably just as well, as the messages are personal to the recipient and most mean little to anyone else, including me.

I do, though, remember one that Keith was given soon after the start of our involvement with Spiritualism. He was doing a driving job at the time and was finding that he was getting headaches – most unusual for him. I advised him many times to go to have his eyes checked, but he always refused as he did not want to wear glasses, so I had told him not to expect any sympathy from me. At one of the services at Bishop Street Spiritualist Church the medium had commented about this eye problem and had advised him to see an optician. The very next day he made an appointment! He was soon wearing glasses, and I was furious that although he had not listened to me he had immediately acted on spirit advice. It just goes to show that good advice does not have to come through spirit or mediums!

I can vividly recall the first public messages I gave. I was very new to the movement then, and was Leader of the Guild at Bishop Street Spiritualist Church. I had by then seen many mediums working, including some nationally known ones.

One night as I lay in bed I wondered what I would do if the medium failed to turn up one day at the Guild. I thought that it would be a good opportunity to see how easy it would be to fake messages, so I thought of some of the regulars and day-dreamed of the messages I could give them, along with 'get-out' phrases that I had heard mediums use.

Not long afterwards this situation actually arose, so I decided to try it out, fully intending to own up at the end. My first message was to a Scottish lady – I described to her a man in a kilt with a tall walking stick striding across the heather. She accepted this. I said I had the name of Alistair, but was not sure if this was <u>his</u> name. I'd heard many mediums say similar things. I was amazed when she said, yes, that was his name! I then went on to describe a grey stone country parish church and its setting amongst trees. Again she recognised it.

That was all I had prepared for her so I went on to the next person. He also accepted everything I said. As did the third person! I hadn't had to use any of my 'get out' ploys! I had only imagined three messages, and when I tried to make something else up on the spot I found that I could not. It seemed that the joke was on me – if I had not thought I was experimenting I would never have had the nerve to stand up and do what I did. The people there were not cross with me - they were just amused by the way that spirit had got me up working!

Subsequently on two occasions (so far) my clairvoyance has failed me. The first time was when I was taking a service as an away medium at a church I had served many times before. This time, however, it was so hard that it felt as though I was wading through treacle. I gave two and a half messages, with great difficulty, before saying I could not go on. Many people there apologised for having brought their problems into the church with them, thus upsetting the vibrations. We had a discussion instead, after which Keith finished with a few messages. It turned out that my chairperson and his wife, who was sitting at the back of the church, were going through a rather acrimonious divorce and it was this that was affecting the energies there, and was also why so many of them charitably claimed responsibility.

This 'failure' actually led to me being booked by another church, a member of which witnessed this. As she said, she knew that I would not fake it whatever, so all my messages could be trusted, unlike some mediums.

The second time something similar happened, at a different church not too long after, the response was quite different – they never booked me again. Would they really have preferred me to make it up?

Keith also had a similar experience once when he struggled to get messages, and that church didn't book him again either. We learnt later that the previous week-end there had been a psychic artist there who must have used up all the available power, which had not had a chance to build up again by the time Keith took their service.

Such 'failures' go to show just how much mediums and clairvoyants are affected by the energies that are in the buildings and that people bring in with them, and so should not be blamed for their lack of inspiration under such conditions. It is not always possible for them to rise above such things, especially when they are new to it. Each session should be regarded as an experiment.

An early message I gave that amazed me was to a man in a church in Stroud. I told him that I was aware of a man in spirit and went on to describe a big black cat that was not a domestic cat, but was a pet the man used to take for walks on a lead. It had very large paws and a long slim tail. I knew I ought to know the name of this type of big cat, but could not recall it, and did not dare risk losing my link trying to do so. He accepted it all, and later told me that the cat I was describing was a panther. Yes, of course – that was the name that had eluded me!

In the autumn of 2002 I gave clairvoyance to a lady at the Beacon of Light Spiritualist Church in Bath. I remembered it because I felt it was particularly good. I was made aware of a Judge from a time long ago when he would not have been called a judge, but would have done the work that nowadays we would consider to be the job of a judge. I gave his name as Denis, remarking that I was being shown that it had one 'n', not the usual two. He was helping her with a long-drawn-out court case to do with family. I gave her the name James, which she said was both her brother and her father, both of whom were involved in this case. I also gave her James Street, which, upon reflection and with surprise, she said was the address of the solicitors. After the service both she and another woman to whom I had given a message said how pleased they were with their messages.

When they learned that I worked in a school they were amazed that someone with such a gift should not be using it full-time. I had to tell them that I was doing good work at the school, and over the years had taken many classes in both Religious Studies and English, talking about life after death, re-incarnation and ghosts, including one based on Charles Dickens' short story 'The Signalman', that I was particularly proud of and which the teacher had 'raved' about later to her departmental head.

Several weeks later I met this lady again at the church. She told me that on relating the message I had given her to a relative who was closely involved, she was shown a family tree by this person showing a long-serving High Sheriff, from the mid fifteenth century, with the family name of Denis (then spelt with one n, later with two)! The lady said that she 'was blown away' by the accuracy of my message – in all honesty, so was I!

More recently I was reminded of a message I had given four years earlier, when I was doing readings at a Mind, Body, & Spirit Fair in Glastonbury's Town Hall, in aid of the Bluebird Appeal children's charity.

Apparently I had, quite correctly, told a woman that she was friendly with a man that she communicated with via the computer. Furthermore I had told her that when her children were grown she would marry the man and move to his country. It seems that her daughter has now started at university, and the previous month she'd married the man and gone to live abroad! How did I know that would happen? I didn't – it was just what my (or her) spirit friends were relaying through me.

Different mediums and clairvoyants work differently, according to their gifts, their spiritual advancement and the influence of their spirit guides and their own personalities. I have found that being clairsentient I pick up messages for people in various ways. I can often feel what the person I am talking to is feeling, whether physically, emotionally or mentally. I am often given symbols to represent certain things, and can usually 'feel' what they mean for that person – the same symbol having different meanings at different times and for different people. Both of these methods mean having to find my own words to describe what I am getting. Sometimes having described it as best I can I find that the person receiving the message does not understand it, or does not accept it. I usually find another way of putting it, resulting in a dawning realisation on the part of the recipient. I learnt early on to actually tell the recipient what symbol I was being given, as on one occasion I tried hard to get a couple to accept a Jewish link, or a link to Israel, with no success until I described to them the Star of David that was being shown to me – whereupon they both immediately knew what it meant. I have also insisted that before I start giving a public message I identify the recipient, never having liked those mediums I have seen who relate something and then ask if anyone can take it. This can result in several people claiming it, and then the medium having to whittle it down to the right one, not always successfully. When I am working in public I also find whilst relaying the message I become aware of my body doing something which leads me into the next bit – e.g. twisting my wedding ring on my finger, or wringing my hands with anxiety. I have found spirit to be very inventive in getting their messages through my limited awareness!

Finally, I would like to share with you an experience I had recently at a small local MBS (Mind, Body, and Spirit) event.

Firstly I must explain that since 1951 we have operated in the UK under the Fraudulent Mediums Act, which replaced the Witchcraft Act of 1735, and which by implication means that the law recognized that there are genuine mediums. However, recently this law has been replaced by one that from April 2008 has put mediums and clairvoyants under the Consumer Protection laws instead. This has led to mediumship and clairvoyance being legally regarded as either 'an experiment' or 'entertainment' where there is any material benefit to the medium or clairvoyant, (e.g. if they charge). The flyer for this particular local event stated 'Please note Readings are purely for entertainment purposes only...'. That may be the law now but it is not what people go to clairvoyants for!

Anyway, I had decided that I would treat myself to a reading, and as I wandered around, relaxing in the friendly atmosphere and looking at the stalls, I observed the clairvoyants in order to decide which one to go to. As I sat drinking a cup of coffee I felt drawn to a lady across the other side of the room, who advertised herself as an international clairvoyant, with a natural gift.

I duly approached her, paid her the money and commented that she was not taping the reading. She replied by showing me a printed disclaimer stating that the readings were purely for entertainment, and saying that she did not make recordings now in case she was later taken to court. This was only a few months after April and people were still coming to terms with the new legislation, so I thought nothing of that, and proceeded to take notes. It turned out to be the most useless reading I had ever had! She got me to shuffle and then chose three cards each from a total of eight different packs of tarot cards, plus throwing three crystals onto a specially made square of cloth. What she said from each of these was not wrong, but just useless, such as (several times) that I was 'a lucky lady'. She did pick up that I was a healer and a clairvoyant myself, although she may already have known this; she said I had someone with me who looked like me, and then waited for me to supply a name, and of the three crystals thrown only one landed on the cloth, from which she said that something would happen in 'five - hours, days, months, years'.

I kept waiting for her to get into her stride and start the real reading, but before I knew it she'd finished, without telling me a single thing worth paying for. I had commented that I thought she could do it without the cards, and she'd replied that, yes she could, but she'd be worn out, and that she had been working all day! What a cop out! Also, halfway through she'd asked me if I was enjoying it – a question that puzzled me until much later when I remembered that it was now all supposed to be purely for entertainment. I don't know how she had the nerve to charge!

I did not express these thoughts as I left feeling totally bemused, a feeling that I later realised had started before I'd had my drink, and that had continued for some hours afterwards. I have since wondered whether she somehow telepathically influences people to come to her, especially perhaps, those with their own power and their guard down, as talking to others I have discovered that they have felt that same pull towards her – although one of my very psychic friends was told by her that "my readings are not for you". I'm sure she had a gift, but she certainly was not using it that time! I have never known or heard of such a lazy reading.

I relate this as a cautionary tale that I hope may put you on your guard and make you think about why you choose particular readers. It also serves to show that even those who, like myself, with some psychic ability, but who are not functioning at that level all of the time, can themselves be fooled. It was indeed a salutary lesson for me!

The following month at a bigger event I went to another tarot card reader, quite new to these events (despite having read the cards for about 20 years), who gave me an excellent reading, and impressed me by not taking my money until after making sure I was satisfied, and who I now recommend to others. When I had first approached her she had done three readings and was taking a break. She had asked me to come back a little later as she needed to recharge, not being used to doing more than one or two at a time. I know it is tiring doing readings all day long, which is why I don't generally do those kind of events, but at least she had been honest about it from the start.

The reader mentioned above was herself disappointed with a reading she paid for recently. She had booked a reading with a man based on his advertising, thinking a shaman would be just the person to help her make some decisions relating to her spiritual path. Even before her appointment arrived she was having doubts, but didn't like to cancel the booking. Afterwards she wished she had, and commented on what a waste of money it was.

A personal recommendation from friends or family is the best, but otherwise do be careful, and learn to trust your own instincts, maybe asking for confirmation of your choice from your own guides.

Spirit Guidance

Keith in 2006

Many years ago, before the days of seat-belts, a friend of ours told us of the time her son had a car accident. Whenever he drove anywhere, she would pray that he be protected. On this particular occasion he'd had a very long day and was tired, but he didn't have much further to drive before he reached home. He must have dozed off for suddenly he found that he had crashed into some bollards; the steering wheel had been pushed right to the back of the driver's seat, but just before that had happened he had felt an unseen force push him across the bench seat onto the passenger side! The police that attended were amazed, as he should have been killed.

Another friend told me of something remarkable that happened to her in the late 1960s. At that time she was living in a house at the end of an unmade lane, with her four children, including a baby. She had been collecting around the affluent houses nearby for the Red Cross, and had finished a long and tiring shift at a more modest house where she had been talking to the man, while his wife listened. The wife gave a very generous donation. Much later she was at home feeling very stressed and in great pain – a pain that she had suffered for many months, when this woman knocked at her door saying she had been told by spirit to come and give her healing. My friend had never heard of healing, and if she hadn't remembered her for that very generous donation she may not have let this stranger in. Apparently this woman had been preparing a meal for her husband when she was told, very insistently, that she needed to go and give healing to a woman who was in dire need of it. She did not know where she lived, but was guided by spirit to her door.

My friend sat on a chair and allowed the woman to place her hands on her head, whereupon she felt a great sense of relief. It was a dull, wet, November day, but the room was suddenly very bright and my friend felt the presence of an angel. The woman put her hand on the exact spot on my friends' back that was causing her problems, and she felt the pain just melt away. How wonderful that help should have been brought to her via a stranger!

Looking back, I can see some of the times and ways that I may have been protected by spirit/angels/God (take your pick).

When I was 16 and working at St George Library, I used to walk to work through the quieter paths of the park. One January morning, when I was almost at the library ready to start work at 9 o'clock, my arm was grabbed by a young man who demanded my purse. He was smartly dressed in a suit, white shirt and a thin sparkly evening style of tie. I just disdainfully looked him up and down, shook my arm free and walked away.

When I went home for lunch I told my mother, who later rang the police, so when I got back to work I had a phone call from the local police station asking me to go down there and give a statement. It turned out that in another Bristol park the previous week this 15 year old had almost raped a girl! At that time I was a quiet mouse of a young woman, so what made me react that way I didn't know – now I believe it to have probably been inspired by my guardian angel - certainly someone was looking out for me.

Not too long afterwards I went on holiday to Sitges, Spain, with my best friend from school. On the second day there we met up with two Spanish boys, who spoke little English and worked as waiters, and whom we then went out with for the remainder of the fortnight. However, on one evening my boy had to work, and they had arranged for someone else to come in his place, so as not to disappoint us. This turned out to be an older man who spoke very good English but with whom I just didn't get on, so after what I thought was a decent interval I said that I would like to go home. We left my friend and her boy enjoying themselves dancing and headed for my hotel – except that when we got to the crossroads my escort said that his hotel was nearer... Oh, my, he'd got the wrong impression! Now what was I going to do? We were arguing in the street and I didn't fancy being picked up by gendarmes, so I reluctantly went to his room. I sat on the edge of his bed (there was nowhere else to sit) as he took off his shirt... Then I noticed that he was glancing at me in a worried kind of way and I realised that I was holding myself across my tummy and rocking backwards and forwards. When he asked if I was alright I said I had a pain in my tummy, so he offered to get me some aspirins. No thanks! He then made me lie down, but as soon as he turned his back I sat up again. With the help of a dictionary, I told him it was my period pain and that I had medication back at the hotel, and then his demeanour changed. He insisted on taking me back to my hotel in his car, which previously had not worked well enough to take us down the coast (thank goodness). The next day he asked my friend how I was, so I must have been convincing. Another piece of good luck? Or a bit of spirit help.

One of my earliest memories of spirit guidance which I recognised as such at the time happened when Beric was a baby. One evening both Keith and I felt a powerful urge to visit Keith's elderly mother – so strong that there was no denying it. We quickly arranged for a neighbour to baby-sit and drove the few miles to her home, where we found her alone, sitting by the fireside. Keith's brother, who lived with her, had gone out. It transpired that the previous day she had fallen down the stairs, badly bruising her legs. She had not told anyone about it, but was sitting there wondering how on earth she was going to get up the stairs to bed that night. She twice refused to allow us to take her to hospital, but Keith's spirit guide eventually spoke through him and told her that "we have ways of making you go". Soon afterwards she agreed to go. This put in motion a series of events that eventually culminated in her being put into a home where her needs could be better met.

In his job as a driver, Keith has benefited from spirit guidance many times. Once, whilst driving a truck he 'saw' a red flash in the corner of his windscreen, so slowed down. If he hadn't he would have crashed into a car that had broken down just around the bend.

On another occasion, in the 1970s, he had to fetch a medium from Bath to take her to Bishop Street Spiritualist Church in Bristol for her to take the service. He was running rather late, but thought he had just enough time to fetch the medium from Bath for the afternoon Guild. He had decided to go via Saltford, but felt inspired to go over Lansdown, however he ignored this and went the way he had planned. He was held up by road works near The Globe Inn for quite some time! Consequently they arrived very late at the church. That taught us not to ignore inspired guidance.

When I had two young children and consequently a much larger figure, I needed some bigger jumpers for winter, but only had enough spare cash for one new one. I was guided to a jumble sale in my local church hall, where I found not one, not two, but six asnu jumpers in my new size – and all for less than the price of one new one! Thank you!

Many years later, soon after I had finished working at Cossham Hospital, Kingswood (where I worked from 1989 to 1991) I was laying in bed one night with Keith asleep beside me when the bedside phone rang. When I answered it a male voice with a beautiful Welsh accent said that he wanted to make love to me. The voice sounded very like a former colleague at Cossham, a very handsome young man, so it was his image which popped into my mind, giving me this mental image of him in bed with a sleeping Keith and me. I just burst out laughing and said something to the effect that I didn't think my husband would like that! Whereupon there was a stunned silence and the caller hung up – he hadn't expected that. (Subsequent investigation convinced me that it was not my lovely Welsh colleague). Once again I now believe that my reaction was guided by spirit.

Spirit friends are only too willing to help with little things as well as the bigger things, provided you ask and are grateful for their help. In about 1980 we had decided to re-decorate our front room to make it into more of a sanctuary-cum-living space. We had very definite ideas of what we wanted, and had looked all over for the wallpaper we wanted with no success. We were about to give up and compromise, when we each, independently, were inspired with the thought of a small local wallpaper shop that we had overlooked, which of course had exactly what we were looking for! We then followed other spirit guidance as to the shops to go to for the items we required. This is how we obtained, with little effort, our carpet and a pair of lamps with rose quartz bases. Our friends seemed very pleased to be involved with the creation of a new atmosphere in this room of ours – it was a team effort!

Since then, I have many times been guided into shops, often charity ones, where I have found books and other items that I have wanted (or books that spirit have wanted me to read) – especially when I have been in no hurry to obtain them.

One book I had bought from *'Cygnus Review'* (an MBS book club) and had lent out, had not been returned, and I was intending to order another copy. One day, due to having a twenty minute gap between changing buses in Bristol, I was able to quickly go into a charity shop I seldom visit, where, much to my surprise, I found a copy of it!

A few years ago I had been thinking that I needed a long coat, not in a dark colour but something that would go with anything, maybe green. Whilst staying with some friends in Axminster, Devon, we lunched in a café on the seafront at Seaton and then visited a charity shop, where, again to my surprise, they had a mint green coat that suited me perfectly. And I hadn't even asked for it – I'd only been thinking about it!

More recently I felt inspired to go to a local village that we seldom go to, although we sometimes drive through it. While Keith looked to see where the MBS event that we had also gone there for was being held I went into the only charity shop I could see. I was just looking at a many-sided pointed pillar of polished crystal when Keith came in. He took it from me and felt such power from it, and such a connection with it, that he wouldn't let it go! It has since helped him many times with difficult cases, under the guidance of Archangel Michael, who was probably the one who guided him to it through my penchant for charity shops.

My sister-in-law Joy sent me this account relating to their dog Katie. *"It happened September 4th 1994. We made a spur of the moment decision to go to Alan and Jeans' and I have always said we were meant to drive up there that day because that is the day we found our Katie wandering abandoned on the hard shoulder of the motorway, we even still had one of Sergeant's leads in the car."* This is not only an example of spirit guidance but also an example of synchronicity, as these two events had to be perfectly synchronised in order to work, with the added bonus of their recently deceased dog's lead still being in the car.

Another example of synchronicity was told to me by my son. He works in Bath as a bus driver, and sometimes goes to a small health food shop a short walk away from the bus station at Widcombe. On one occasion he was just leaving the shop when a woman came in asking if they had a *'Positive News'*. The shop keepers had never heard of this free newspaper which focuses entirely on the positive happenings in the world, but my son was able to tell them about it. He subsequently took an old copy in for them to see. Some time later he took in a couple of copies of the latest edition during the twenty minute break he had. Whilst there a customer commented that she hadn't seen them since she'd moved to Bath from Scotland, and took details. As a consequence of these two synchronicities (which I know some people would call co-incidences) the shop has decided to stock them.

Another friend told me of this encounter. In the summer of 2001 at 2 a.m. he was mugged by three young men as he was walking home. They knocked him to the ground and took his bag. However, someone was looking after him because he saw a tall dark shape standing over him, which these men must also have seen, because they dropped his bag, and their own, and ran away in terror calling "please don't hurt us" (or something to that effect). The police found their diary in their bag.

In July 2006, Keith and I were booked to take the Sunday service at a church over 60 miles away. It was only our third visit to this church, the previous two having been in the autumn and winter months. During the morning, I was guided to a reading about angels from the White Eagle book *'Walking With Angels'*. We set off in plenty of time in case of delays but having no problems we got there with time to spare, so we parked up a couple of miles away at Dunster Castle, a National Trust property. It was a beautifully sunny afternoon and we picnicked in the grassy car-park.

All day I had felt that I wanted to take the whole service, and as Keith was agreeable to this we decided that I should. We arrived at the church at 2.50 p.m. ready to take the 3 o'clock service, only to find it locked – it transpired that the summer services were held at 6.30! With 3½ hours to spare, and no food, we drove back to the spot we had been parked in shortly before and found some sustenance in the nearby village. We then rested in the car.

At around 5.30 p.m. I asked out loud for anyone who could hear me, other than Keith, to come to me, because if they could hear me it meant they were what the world calls 'dead' and unless they could come and go at will we would be able to help them get to where they were meant to be.

The gates of the car-park were closed at 6 p.m. so we left there by then and I took the service as planned. During the clairvoyance I went to three young ladies with a message concerned that they should stick together despite anything that tried to part them. Afterwards they approached me with their situation. One of the young ladies, Anne, was a devout Baptist who had a very strong belief that the Holy Spirit was with her, and she had for a long time been aware of a protective presence in her home.

Recently, however, another young woman who had previously only ever been in her garden had entered her house. The atmosphere in the house suddenly changed, and Anne 'saw' a child run to her as if for protection. Since then the child was there, but also a man who was friendly to the children and herself, but was at other times "evil". It transpired that the friend who had started all this off when she entered the house - a house that had actually been transformed into a sacred space by the holy activities within - had six months previously been using a homemade ouija board. The protective spirit was just not strong enough to cope with what had been separated from this woman by the powerful light in the house.

Her friend's mother had suggested that they come to the "spiritual" church, but Anne was unsure – she only decided to come at 5.35 p.m. that day – just after I had been inviting lost souls to come to me.

Not being local we did not know if there was anyone nearby who could deal with this, so we arranged to go to her home with her from the church. The man/child hid from us at first, but we persevered and found that they were afraid of other lost souls who were bullying them. (The same soul appeared in either the form of a child or of a man - rather confusing!). We succeeded in getting all the souls to go to the light.

If you look more closely at this story, you will see just how much was involved in the form of spirit guidance – if we hadn't got the time of the service wrong, we would not have had time to spare so I would not have sent out my thoughts to the lost souls, and maybe Anne and her friends would not have come to the church that night. Also, my feeling that I wanted to take the whole service meant that Keith saved his energy for the later task. On top of that, my reading about angels resonated with these rather unsure new members of the congregation.

A wonderful example of spirit guidance occurred one summer weekend some years ago. Keith wanted us to go out for a walk on the Saturday, but couldn't decide where. We agreed on somewhere along the Ridgeway, but as this is a mighty long ancient trackway we had to decide which bit to do. Keith wanted to do the western end of it; I wanted to include Wayland's Smithy, an ancient monument which I had never visited. I went to see a friend and borrowed a book of walks from him that included one for the Smithy, but we could find none that included the end of the Ridgeway, only an OS map.

On the morning of the Saturday we still had not decided but as Keith was getting grumpy I told him I would leave it to him. He decided to do the walk I wanted so we duly set off, looking forward to a leisurely day. We were in no hurry so we planned to use the minor roads to get there rather than the motorway.

However, spirit had other ideas and impressed Keith to use the motorway. On being asked why they said we were in a hurry and had to be there by noon. Keith said that was pushing it and we'd never make it - whereupon something made me say "noon by the sun, not by the clock", which was an hour later.

Anyway, we got onto the Ridgeway about 10 minutes before noon. We proceeded to saunter along, stopping to look at and smell the flowers, but spirit hurried us up again. The Ridgeway is classed as a green road which means it is only open to vehicles at certain times. A couple of cars passed us and we could see in the distance, by a copse, more vehicles and people who as we got nearer appeared to be wearing costume. We thought they must be filming something but we saw no such equipment.

As we got nearer still, we realised that the copse was the stand of trees around Wayland's Smithy. Access was by a narrow lane, two persons wide. As we turned into this lane there were six people there and I heard one of them say "let's process in". We tagged on the end and so 'processed in' to what turned out to be a handfasting – a pagan wedding!

We felt very privileged to be able to witness this from beginning to end. We saw the sacred space opened up, witnessed the whole ceremony, and were invited at the end to partake of the bread and mead (previously prepared by the bride and groom respectively) as part of the ceremony. We were then invited to stay for the celebrations which included food sharing. We had only brought sandwiches which hardly seemed appropriate but there was plenty of food to go round and we were made very welcome. We felt we should offer the happy couple some gift – money didn't seem right, so I offered them the only suitable thing that we had with us - a small carnelian crystal.

It was a fantastic experience which we would have missed if we had not followed the guidance of our spirit friends.

One evening in July 2007, a tall man giving his name as Sam spoke through Keith in our front room. It seems he had been inspiring Keith for some time but had never spoken through him before. He was trying to speak through him when Keith had his eyes open, as this is how Keith wanted to work when he did clairvoyance.

In answer to my questions Sam said he was last alive on this earth about the turn of the last century, i.e. 1900, in Britain. Sam said that in a past life he lived in Bristol and knew Edward Colston whom he considered to be a good man. He said that he had been in W's house with us when we visited recently - Colston Villa, on the site of Edward Colston's house - and noticed how different it is there now. *[Edward Colston was a very successful merchant, born in Bristol in 1636, and was a great benefactor of the city. These days he is often decried as a slave trader but he had already made his fame and fortune by the time he first started trading in slaves, which in any case in his day was considered an acceptable form of trading. Keith is descended from one of his brothers, he himself having been childless].*

When Beric came into the room, Sam advised him to "take it steady" tomorrow on his way to Southampton, on the road past Salisbury, before he gets onto the M27. He narrowed this down, on being questioned, to the roundabout before the motorway, and said it was not something natural like flooding or an animal, but something to do with the road vehicles. He said Beric would be safe, but just to be aware and take it steady.

The following day, at that roundabout, Beric says there was an oil residue right across the carriageway, probably diesel, which would have been slippery. He could not avoid driving right through it, getting it on all four tyres of his van. Beric was helping a friend move to Birmingham to be with her partner. Sam also said that this friend would have another baby girl next June – she already has two. When Beric told her this, she was stunned as they don't plan to have another baby until the following year, and in the meantime she has an implant to prevent conception. *[She didn't – which just goes to show that spirit are fallible too, especially with regard to time].*

Sam also took the opportunity to introduce me to Jonathan, who said he had been working with me for a few years now. Jonathan said that later this year things would start to happen to me that would take me in another direction - four things, maybe like four steps. In answer to my questions, it appears that soon something will be set in motion relating to my book, and that Jonathan helped me write it and will help me write the next one. *(This refers to the previous incarnation of this book, of which I'd had 40 copies printed by a friend in December 2006, just in time for Christmas – it was almost a third the size of this one – I'd had a further 50 printed later).* In October 2007 I finally gave up home visits as I could no longer sustain them – step one maybe? This has led me to spending more time on myself – the 'me time' I have not had much of for so many years, and so was able to expand my book by about two-thirds – which may have been step two. Step three may have been me contacting a literary agency with whom I signed up in May 2009. Step four then followed as a result of this when I divided my much-expanded book into three sections, and re-arranged each of the main chapters to be more chronological.

Spirit guidance can be given through a third party. Our good friend Mairi gave me a letter to hold from one of her relatives in Scotland and asked if I could give her some advice. This relative was a part-time crofter and sheep breeder which had left her with severe back problems and arthritic hands. She was also a school cook, working alone, was finding the job very stressful, and her health was suffering. On top of this she had a job as a market researcher to supplement her income. She wanted to give up her cooks' job but was afraid that she might not be able to get work because of her poor health.

I asked for spirits' help and was advised that she should give up her job either at the end of the term, or the school year, and that something would come up via her market research connection that would make sure she was okay. Following this advice she decided to "go for it" and so gave up her job at Easter, since when she has had plenty of work offers for market research both locally and farther afield (she has made several trips to the Orkneys), where her experience and contacts as a crofter and sheep breeder have been especially valued.

Her health has greatly improved and she is now so happy and well that she wonders how she coped before. In addition she has also been granted an unexpected pension by the school in recognition for her 32 years service! Within a year she was so busy that she even had to turn down two or three market research contracts! She told Mairi that she rated my advice as "110% accurate" and was most impressed and grateful.

Back in 2004 Keith and I had been asked by our friend Charlie to have a weekly healing session above the carpet shop of a friend of his in Bedminster, Bristol. The upstairs room was made available and Harry (another friend of both Charlie and the shop manager) put in many hours of hard work to get it ready and in a fit state for us to use, including a toilet - paying for much of it from his own pocket. We ran it for a little while as the Rainbow Centre, also a monthly meditation group, but neither were overly successful and we left soon after the room also became used by Hare Krishna devotees, who introduced a very different vibration to the space which did not harmonize with us. Harry then offered us the use of his home near the Cumberland Basin, which he made into a lovely little 'church' for services, healing and meditation. Again, as Stardust, it ran for only a little while, maybe two years. We did meet a couple that we are still giving healing to and a lady who has recently come back into our lives, who later gave me an excellent tarot reading, and who has now (2011) joined us as a healer at our Drop-in Healing Clinic.

We saw little of Harry after that until one day in October 2008 we met someone at our clinic in Fishponds that Keith had given healing to during that time. This man told us that Harry had a singing engagement the following Wednesday at a hotel in Clifton, and insisted that we write down the details and go there - which we did, as we had never heard Harry sing professionally. It was the first time that Harry had sung there (or anywhere professionally for some time). We arrived early not knowing when he would be on. He wasn't on 'til 9 p.m. but he'd stayed around wondering what to do – should he go home? He was amazed to see us, and we spent an hour or so talking before his gig. A few days later he gave us a ring to ask for our healing thoughts for someone.

In the meantime we were trying to contact an old colleague of mine from work who had helped us a few years before with decorating, following a mini-tornado and the subsequent discovery of our dangerous electrics and their total replacement. *[See next chapter]*. No-one was answering his phone. We had reached the stage when we needed someone to fit our stair carpet. It suddenly dawned on me (or was the memory called up for me?) that Harry used to help out sometimes with carpet laying! It had obviously been arranged for us to get back in touch with him just when we needed his skills! He also, it turned out, had needed to be put back in touch with us so that he could bring people (or send them) to our healing clinic!

In October 2009 Keith's sister Joy, had arranged with her sister-in-law, Jean, that Jean would visit her the next day. Jean would catch a train from Gloucester, that Joy and her daughter Sally would meet at the station at the usual time (10.30 a.m.). During the night Joy's elderly dog became very poorly, and Joy and Sally sat up all night with him. In the morning they arranged an appointment with the vet at 11 a.m. This meant they would not be able to meet the train, so Joy rang Jean at 8.40 a.m. to amend the arrangements, only to be told by her husband that she was on the train now and that he'd rushed her out of the house otherwise she would have missed it – the usual one, 8.42. That was not the usual one, but it did allow Joy to meet the train, which arrived at 9.30. No-one could explain how he'd got it into his head that her usual train was at 8.42, not 9.42. He'd rushed her so much that it hadn't occurred to her until she was on the train! But it turned out to be a much better journey on the earlier train, so she'll catch that in future.

Later, Joy opened a kitchen wall cupboard, from the top of which a container fell into Jean's arms - a container that we had borrowed at a family celebration in Gloucester and given to Joy some time before to return to Jean.

A fortnight later, at the end of October, Jean visited Joy again. She picked up a *People's Friend* magazine from August to read on the train – unbeknown to her it was the very one Joy was missing for the serial in it.

These are the kind of 'coincidences' that many people do not recognize as being guidance and help from spirit friends/angels/the Higher Self/the Universe (whichever). Personally, I love these synchronicities.

A scientifically-minded friend of mine, who had moved to his dream cottage with wooded grounds and streams - with the aid of a loan from another friend - once asked me to show him a miracle – just a little one would do – so that he might have some evidence of the things I believe. I told him he'd already had his miracle, and not just a little one at that, as I indicated his new home, which not too long before had seemed totally unobtainable. That made him think!

Mysterious Ways

Me between my two pregnancies

Between my two pregnancies I worked for a season front of house at the Bristol Old Vic.

I soon discovered that the bus to take me in was always late because of the rush hour traffic it had to come through on the way out. Consequently a colleague, who lived at Stockwood and delivered paints around the south-west during the day, offered to fetch and carry me. One night I had a very vivid dream – this man and I were walking down the short street I grew up on. When we reached the bottom we saw a procession of vehicles coming up the hill of the adjoining road. There were three ambulances and a Sparrow Crane Hire vehicle. I said, "There seems to have been an accident". My companion appeared to know all about it, and the scene changed. I saw, in this dream, a bridge high above a stream or river, then I saw the bridge fall away and two cars go over the edge. The other cars stopped on the dual carriageway which was separated from the other carriageway by a raised pavement. They had nowhere to go. In the dream my companion took me to the bridge and showed me the steel girders that it was made of and how some were loose.

I told him and Keith about this weird dream and then forgot about it.

About a fortnight later my colleague rang me from Bridgwater to say he would not be able to pick me up as he would be late. There had been an accident on the dual carriageway and he was stuck in the traffic. Whilst coming around a corner a lorry carrying steel girders had shed its load, crushing two cars and killing three people. The traffic had nowhere to go and just had to wait until a Sparrow Crane Hire vehicle arrived to move the girders. So my dream was precognitive!

It had foretold 8 items: –

- Bridgwater (the bridge over the water)
- Two cars destroyed
- Three people hurt (the three ambulances)
- The steel girders that were loose
- The dual carriageway
- The raised pavement preventing traffic from turning
- The Sparrow Crane Hire vehicle
- The fact that my colleague knew all about it.

Yet that lorry could not even have been loaded at the time of my dream – my mind still boggles at the implications!

Many years ago whilst we were still at Bishop Street Spiritualist Church we knew a man, Frank, who told us he'd had a vision in October 1966 of a South Wales school that had been buried under coal waste. He had spent a whole day going around the Welsh valleys looking at all the schools. By the end of that Friday he had made a shortlist of three schools that had slag heaps looming over them which matched his vision. He had thought of going to the Head Teachers to tell them of the danger, but was tired and decided to go home, rest, and come back the following Monday. By then it was too late, as the school at Aberfan, one of those on his list, had been engulfed by the coal waste, killing 144 people, mainly children. He never forgave himself, but as I said to him, even if he had told the Head Teachers, and even if they had believed him and acted upon it, it would probably still have happened as I doubt they would have been able to have acted in time.

In June 1982 we were on our way to the funeral in Nottingham of Alf, one of our church members, with several others from the church in our minibus. As we drove towards the M4 Keith was being told to 'go the old road', but he ignored this advice because he thought it would be quicker on the motorway. However, as we approached the sliproad on the M4 for the A46, the engine just died and it would not restart. Keith called out the AA and we waited on the hard shoulder for them to arrive. When they tried to start the engine it sprang into life immediately, and gave us no further trouble. Why did this happen? Were we meant to be later to avoid an accident? Who knows? One of life's mysteries.

At that time the minibus was being maintained for free by another member of our church, Bob, because we used it so much for the church. When Keith parked up at Hambrook to drive the lorry Bob would go there and work on the minibus. One such time Charlie had told him that he felt there was a problem with the wheel so he had a good look but could find nothing wrong. He knew Charlie was a good clairvoyant therefore there must be something wrong, so he went round the wheels again, but could still not find a problem. He stood quietly and asked for spirit help – whereupon he was 'shown' a wheel arch. When he looked up under the front wheel arch he found a large stone lodged against the steering mechanism. If it had not been removed then the wheels may not have turned enough and may therefore have caused an accident. There was no way any living person could have known of this problem. (People often quote telepathy to explain spirit messages, or co-incidence, it was neither of those.) Thank you, spirit friends!

On July 12th 1994 Keith and I went to a photographic exhibition on the top floor of the two storey building of our local village hall. It was a beautiful summer's day, and as we left the exhibition on their outside steps we saw the beautiful blue cloudless sky - cloudless, that is, except for some white clouds just above the horizon. Looking out above the houses we were amazed to see large fluffy white clouds spelling out - in totally separate letters - 'ZION' between two lines of horizontal clouds! It was nothing like sky-writing. Unfortunately we had no camera with us, and we just knew that by the time we could have got one the formation would have disappeared.

Back in 1996 Keith had a car accident. On his birthday in May, he had gone to work and afterwards gone directly to take a service in Stonehouse, Gloucestershire. I was ill in bed otherwise he would have picked me up on his way through. He didn't return home again for 10 days, having broken both arms! The collision had occurred in pouring rain – so bad that many vehicles were pulling over rather than drive in it. Our car had been damaged at both ends and stuff from inside both the bonnet and the boot was found scattered in the hedgerow and surrounding fields on both sides of the road, although the roof of the car was not damaged. The driver behind had a mobile phone (rare back then) and first aid training, so help was quickly called for and given. A fatal accident unit was sent – but no-one died.

I arranged to have compassionate leave from work, as I envisaged him coming home with both arms in plaster. However I didn't need it, as he came home instead with metal pins in both arms.

The previous year it had been foretold to our friend Charlie, when a seaside clairvoyant had said that "a good friend would have an accident that was not his fault. He would be hurt, but he would be okay, and it wouldn't happen for a year". And the birthday present I had bought months before was exactly what he needed – a silky dressing gown! He only had a heavy terry towelling one that would not have been suitable – too heavy, and it would have caught on the stitches.

It obviously had to happen for some reason but the angels were with him to help as much as possible. It eventually led to him giving up work and taking over all the household chores instead, thus helping me as many of those chores made my back hurt where it had been damaged on the Norfolk Broads. *[See Chapter 14 - Healing]*.

In 1999, whilst regularly travelling by bus to and from Bath, Keith became aware of a different sort of energy every time he went through the village of Kelston, an energy he could not identify. Then one day he heard some schoolgirls talking of the crop circles that had appeared. Upon investigation we saw some circles in a field of oil-seed rape in beautiful full yellow bloom – the variously sized circles stood out because you could clearly see the green stalks of the plants left standing around the edges of the flattened yellow circles.

In view of the energies Keith had felt we believed them to be genuine, but a couple of weeks later there was no doubt at all as the field had turned green when the flowers had faded from the rest of the field - the only ones still yellow were the ones that had been laid flat within the circles!

In 2004, before we went on holiday, we obtained a quote for the renewal of our old and decaying conservatory and the roof of the garage. We said that when we returned, we would fix a date for the work to be done. However …

We arrived at Vegan Camp 2004 in Northumberland on the Saturday. On the Monday we had taken two other campers with us to visit some castles. At the last one it had poured with rain and the last two of us back to the car had got soaked through. After turning off the M1 onto the road leading to the campsite (a good road, mostly straight), we approached a bend that was marked with the S–bend sign. Keith slowed, expecting a bend of about 60 degrees. By the time he realised that it was a 90 degree turn we were going too fast and the wet road and a large pot-hole stopped us from slowing more. We managed about 80 degrees, which took us across the road and head on into the end of a hedge, after first demolishing a wooden fence with a sideways swipe - a new fence which had obviously been put there as a result of previous accidents.

Fortunately the angels were with us, as nothing was coming the other way (they would not have had time to avoid us) and no-one was hurt except me. I had braced myself for impact with my hands on the dashboard but had removed my hands just in time when I felt a sharp pain at the base of my right thumb. Otherwise I am sure I would have had broken bones. The two people in the back seat hadn't realised anything was wrong until the impact.

Whilst Keith phoned our insurers our friend rang the camp who sent out a rescue vehicle. (Thank God for mobile phones!). Several people stopped to offer help but we told them we were OK – until I recognised the voice of a friend from Bristol! He had just dropped another friend off at camp before going to check in at a guesthouse and had driven past what he thought was an abandoned car. Realising he had gone too far he was driving back to find his guesthouse when he realised there were people in the car and so stopped to offer help. Imagine his surprise when, so far from home, on his first day in a county he had never before visited, he found his name being called from an occupant of a crashed car!

He took the three of us back to camp, leaving the driver of the rescue vehicle from camp to stay with Keith until help arrived – four hours later. He also took some food and drink to the two of them on his way back to his guesthouse. More help from the angels.

Our old car was an economic write-off, so we had to spend the money for the conservatory/garage roof on a new car instead.

Our old and new cars outside our home

On returning from holiday I e-mailed a strongly-worded complaint to the Northumberland County Council and five days later they replied that they would put slow markings on the road, put up warning chevrons and send someone to look at the pothole. So, maybe, someone who would otherwise have been killed or seriously injured will now be spared.

Fast forward from August to January.

On our return home after spending Christmas 2004 and New Year with our daughter in Surrey, we found that whilst we were all away our home in Oldland Common, South Gloucestershire, along with two dozen others and the primary school, had been hit by a mini-tornado! (This was in the week following the Boxing Day Asian tsunami). A large tree had also been torn up and thrown across the main road.

Fortunately at our house the tornado was not at ground level as nothing from the garden had been affected. Five ridge tiles from the roof had been torn off, had damaged two others on their way down, then one had gone through the garage roof and one had broken the roof of the conservatory. Both of which would have been new if it hadn't been for the accident!

When, eventually, the insurers authorised the repairs, we had a more substantial garage roof fitted – for which they had to switch off the electrics. In so doing they found some of the cables had melted, and that our electrics were in a dangerous state. Some of the wiring was 50 years old, some about 30 years, so it was due for an overhaul. That meant clearing the whole house of 35 years of living, including the bringing up of two children, so that it could be done – including the loft.

Now, the loft was in need of more insulation. In February the previous year we had applied for a grant for this, and had been told that we would be top of the list in April. Nothing happened. The following February we asked again, and have now had it done, BUT if it had been done the previous year it would have had to have been removed again for the electricians to rewire the upstairs lights! So someone up there knew what was coming. Also we found that some of the beams had some woodworm in – so that was treated first, too.

Following the re-wiring, the house needed almost total redecoration.

I leave you to imagine the stress involved in all of this – if it had happened the previous year, when I was still at work, I just would not have been able to cope.

In 2005 Keith and I travelled to Essex to take the funeral of a dear friend after which we went back with the family to her home. The following mysterious thing happened:-

After the ceremony, in the Hall, I slung my handbag over my shoulder and felt and heard my clip-on ear-ring come off. I did not hear it hit the floor or a chair, and several of us could not find it anywhere in that sparsely furnished Hall. Rosie watched as I took everything from my right blazer pocket – car-keys; a pendant on a chain; and a medallion – there was nothing else. I took the remaining sapphire and diamond ear-ring off, closed it, and put it in my left blazer pocket. Rosie looked in my hair etc – she even made me take my blazer off and shake it!

Back at the house I showed the son of the deceased the remaining ear-ring, putting it back in the same left-hand pocket, and I again went through my pockets and my bag – nothing. Before we left I used the toilet and stood well clear as I dropped my trousers, just in case. Afterwards as I lifted my blouse to re-fasten my trousers, an open ear-ring dropped to the ground. Yes!! Well, no, actually. As I reached into my left-hand pocket for the other one – it wasn't there! I checked all my pockets again, taking everything out, and there was no other ear-ring. How it could have fallen on the floor open I do not know as they are not easy to open, and it was definitely closed in my pocket, and it shouldn't have been able to fall out of that pocket anyway.

Several hours later when we got back home I emptied both pockets onto the dressing table, and was amazed to find I had an ear-ring in each of my blazer pockets. What happened I will never know, only that for several hours that afternoon one ear-ring completely disappeared, only to re-appear as if nothing had happened.

A similar thing had happened in the winter of 2001 when I broke my wrist, *[see Chapter 10 – Animal Tales]*. As it was my left wrist I had taken my wedding ring and watch off before the swelling set in. I put them in a pocket and thought nothing of them for quite some time. Then I retrieved the wedding ring, which I could no longer wear, and put it away. I could not find the watch. I looked in all the pockets of all the clothes I had been wearing that day, to no avail. I did this several times, as it <u>had</u> to be in there somewhere. Months went by, the seasons came and went, and soon it was autumn. I got out the gilet I had been wearing when I broke my wrist, and lo and behold, the watch was in the pocket! Of a garment I had searched several times!

Relating this tale to my friend Doreen, she told me of the time she went looking for her husband in their large three-storey Victorian house. She searched everywhere for him, including the cellar. When she asked him where he'd been all that time, he was adamant that he'd spent the whole time in his study. It seems that, like some of the stuck spirits, we can sometimes go into a different dimension to usual, and thus become invisible to those in the normal world. As can our belongings.

Only last month, Keith was looking for his pen that he keeps on his small table. I watched as he looked, and saw him pick up and shake a small pile of papers – nothing. I continued to watch as he looked under another pile – nothing. Then just as he stood back, baffled, we both saw the pen on the edge of the first pile that he had picked up and shaken! We both swear that it was not there just a few seconds previously!

Recently my daughter told me of one of her colleagues who came into work and had told her of a strange dream she'd had that night. She had dreamt that she was in their department store looking unsuccessfully for a plum coloured coat in her size, with the Betty Jackson label. There was no such coat in stock, but the following day they came in, and the style and colour were exactly as she had dreamt it, right down to the buttons! My daughter was amused but her colleague was spooked.

Healing

Me at a BDAH healing stall 2005

I'm not sure that this comes under the heading of the paranormal, as the results can often be assessed by normal, objective, scientific means, although the mechanism used in the process is still beyond the scope of most scientists' understanding. It is only just beginning to be understood in the realms of quantum physics – see the book 'The Field' by Lynne McTaggart, first published by HarperCollins in 2001.

When I was at Library School in Ealing in the late 1960s I was a member of the college sailing club. On a club trip on an eight-berth sailing barge on the Norfolk Broads, we were moored and I was standing alone on the deck when the wind blew the sail up along with its very long and heavy wooden boom, causing it's support to fall away and the boom to come down smack on my head. I found out much later that the shock had travelled all the way down my spine and pushed the lower three vertebrae together. If it had hit me at an angle it would probably have broken my neck. From then on I found it very painful to straighten up after bending over, so I used to wash my long hair in the bath instead of over the sink, otherwise I would have to lie on the bed in pain for ages afterwards whilst my back re-adjusted itself. But I got used to it and it hindered me very little.

When we first became involved with Spiritualism, I began to have healing at the Bishop Street Church from Mr Ted Lester. On one occasion his hands went further down my back than hitherto and I felt the tail of my spine kick, as did he. This re-started the whole problem, but after many weeks of healing I found that I could bend over the sink to wash my hair once again with very little discomfort. Although it will always be a weak spot, and I do work around it, it has caused me very little trouble since.

The same accident caused me to develop a tendency towards migraines, which peaked in 1994 when I suffered 17 migraines, each one lasting a week – three days of intense pain and forced inactivity, followed by three days of recuperation. Prior to that I had ascertained that many of my migraines were the result of allergies – cheese, chocolate, sherry, cigarette smoke, certain paint fumes … The 1994 ones were mainly due, it turned out, to the hair colourant I was using to disguise my increasingly grey hair – oh the price of vanity!

Some years later, when we were due to have a stall at a Mind, Body, Spirit event, I decided that I would treat myself to a therapy session. I studied the programme, and attended a workshop by Tarpan Williams of Spineworks. He had studied many therapies and had evolved a system of his own which utilised spots on the body that he termed "cellulomes"; these often corresponded to acupuncture points, but also included others. I decided to go to him for treatment to my left shoulder which was playing up because of my work on computers. However, he tuned into my migraines!

I lay on the couch while he gently but firmly pressed his fingers into two points on the back of my neck, and I told him of the feelings that I was aware of throughout my body. It was meant to be a 15 minute session, but when I stood up it was an hour later! He said I might get one last very bad migraine. I said "Last?", whereupon he said I should not get any more. I responded by saying that if it was the last I didn't care how bad it was. However I never did get that very bad last migraine, but although I do still get migraines they are now <u>very much</u> less frequent and involve only one day of pain and one day getting over it. It was the best £15 I've ever spent! Before I got around to visiting him again, at his place in Swindon, I heard that he had returned to his native Australia.

When the children were small I took them on a peaceful demonstration on the Downs. A metal tent pole supporting a banner came loose and struck me a blow just above my left eye, making me reel. I was concerned that I might develop a headache from it that would jeopardise my care of my two young children, so I sent out a quick plea to spirit for help. I was aware of a flash of white light in the affected area, and then it was as if it had never happened. No pain, no bruising, nothing. I was amazed!

One of our first patients was our next-door neighbour. She had lost her husband some years before and had since developed a hearing problem. Whilst chatting one day she told me she had spent £84 (I think it was – and this was in the mid 1970s) on a hearing aid her doctor had told her would not work. She was so desperate she just had to try it. It didn't work, and she was at her wits end. She had stopped walking to the Post Office, a quarter of a mile away, because people would stop and talk to her and she couldn't hear what they were saying – it was embarrassing. She also could not hear her doorbell ring, and only sometimes the phone and when she answered it she might not be able to hear what they were saying, even to know who they were. Also, when she went to bed at night she couldn't sleep, because then she would get a pounding in her ears that kept her awake.

I asked her if she had ever thought of trying healing, to which she replied with a shrug, "well, yes, but where would I go?" She was amazed when I said, "to us".

She came weekly for the next 18 months or so. After the first session she told us that the pounding in her ears at night had stopped, so she was now sleeping. That made a big difference to her. She also suffered from arthritis, to the extent that sometimes she could not grip things, and oft-times would sit on her hands in an effort to relieve the pain.

By the time she stopped coming regularly, she could hear enough to be able to interact socially again, and only got a twinge in her hands "when the weather changed". Her directional hearing was still not good – she could for instance now hear a dog barking, but not know where it was coming from.

She often said at the end of a session that she felt so relaxed she just wanted to go home and go to sleep. This is a common feeling which is very beneficial to succumb to. She also said she couldn't get away with anything as we always picked up on any other health problem she came with whether she mentioned it or not – e.g. a painful back from exerting herself in the garden.

This led on to another patient who heard of this. He was the husband of a woman who worked in a local supermarket - a heating engineer who had been off work for months. He had a slipped disc, which the doctors could do no more for than give him painkillers which, by his own admission, he "ate like Smarties". He said when he looked in the mirror he could see that he went down to the hips, then sideways and down again. It didn't really show much, but it must have been excruciatingly painful. He had taken to sleeping on the floor alongside the marital bed as the bed was too soft and even more painful than the floor. He didn't really sleep, though, and in the middle of the night he would get up, take some more painkillers, wander about until they started to take effect, and then go and lie down again. He was also at his wits end, and came into our front room and sat on the stool as if to say 'do your worst, it can't be any worse than this'. We channelled healing to him, which was easy as he just soaked it up, and told him that from our experience he could expect a good night's sleep that night, and we arranged for him to return the following week.

The next week when he walked in the door he looked so much better. He told us he had slept "like a log" every night that week, and so had cut his intake of painkillers in half.

The following week he was jumping up and down for joy. "I keep looking in the mirror", he said, "I'm straight, I'm straight". Before he came again, he rang to say he'd had the offer of a job and asked us if he should take it. It would involve crawling around in attics and small spaces, but he said he felt he could do it, so we said be careful, wear your surgical belt, but if you feel up to it go ahead. He came for healing a few more times just to make sure of it, and we haven't seen him since.

As a consequence of this wonderful result, his wife's manager came to see us. He too had a bad back, but for a different reason. As he sat on the stool we realised that he was not absorbing the healing energies. Keith was aware of them bouncing off. Try as we might, and as he might, we could not get him to relax sufficiently for the healing energies to flow into him. It wasn't that he didn't trust us, or that he didn't want to get better, it was just that he had a very analytical mind and could not switch it off. There really is not much to see whilst someone is receiving healing (unless you happen to be clairvoyant, Keith can sometimes see the energy). We told him to just mentally note what was happening, but to leave the analysis until later, but he couldn't, so eventually we had to both admit defeat.

The energies flowing through us have got more powerful since then, and of course we have learnt more, so maybe today if he had come it would have been different.

In January 1983 I had treated another friend of mine, who was waiting for an operation for a very painful ingrown toe-nail. As she sat on her bed I held my hands around her toes, without touching. She said she could feel the big toe and the one next to it freezing, but not the others. I could feel my left hand freezing – so afterwards I sent a thought to my spirit helpers saying, "I know you must have a good reason for freezing the toes, but do you have to freeze my hand as well?"

The following week when I gave treatment, my friend's toes froze as before, but my hand didn't.

A smaller success was with a friend who had sprained his ankle playing football. He was an interested sceptic so accepted my offer of healing, more from curiosity and politeness I think than anything. I held my hands around his injury, again without touching, for quite some time. When I felt the power cease to flow I was puzzled because I could not move my hands away for several minutes. Afterwards my friend said that during the healing it felt as if things were moving around inside his foot. He also said he knew that the healing had ceased long before I removed my hands. I assume it happened in order for him to be more convinced by what he felt.

When my youngest was still at primary school, [1985] I was friendly with a neighbour who suffered with a very bad back. She had three young children, all at school, but spent most of the day lying on the settee. She had to have someone else do most of her housework. After some time of regular weekly treatments she got so much better that she not only was able to do her own housework, but got a job doing someone else's. I commented on this once, saying that here was me who couldn't find such a job, and needing one to bring in a bit of extra cash! She said if I wanted one she knew a lady who needed someone. That's how I came to clean for a while for a business woman with two children and Alsatian dogs.

We never charge for healing, but we will always accept donations. Some people give nothing, some a pound or two, others donate £10 or more and yet others repay us in kind. On one occasion we were given a weekend on a friend's yacht, with him of course, at Dartmouth. That was a glorious weekend! We have also been loaned a car for a week when ours broke down just before we were due to go on holiday.

Fortunately it had an accessory that ours didn't, as when we were just about to leave a grateful patient turned up with a bunch of flowers for us, which we were able to take with us in the stick-on vase attached to the dashboard!

We had a wealthy patient once, back in the 1970s, who used to give us £10 every time he visited us with his wife. When they found we were saving it in a separate account to spend for things for our church, they began to give us £10 plus a bunch of flowers, or a cabbage or something we had to use for ourselves. This was very much appreciated, as money was tight at that time.

On June 13th 1986 my mother was taken into Manor Park Hospital after suffering a series of violent shaking attacks, some lasting 45 minutes, over a period of three weeks, which the doctors later called mini-strokes. She was put on a drip as she was so dehydrated, and had been refusing food and drink. She was taken off the drip, but had to be put back on it a few days later.

She didn't look like my Mum any more, just very pale and like any other old lady who was very near the end of her life. My Dad was like a little boy lost at the thought of being without her after 53 years of marriage. The doctor had told us he could find nothing wrong with her, so when Keith and I visited her midday on the 19th I sat holding both her hand and Keith's hand as we tried to channel healing into her. I talked to her telling her the doctors could find nothing wrong with her, and she didn't have to leave us; she was only 77 and could choose to stay with us if she wanted to; how Dad would miss her, etc. As I was doing this Keith could see her spirit half out of her body - a haze of energy floating just above her, overlapping her prone body. He linked in telepathically telling her she could pass on or stay with her family, whichever she wanted.

We really thought we would get a call in the night telling us she had passed on, but it didn't come. The next day when we went in we were amazed to see her in her chair having the drip taken off! She must have heard us and decided to stay with us a bit longer – six years longer as it turned out! I have written in my diary for that day, *"Apparently the case baffles the staff"*.

Another experience of note was with a friend and colleague who had suffered years of trouble with her back, since being involved in a road accident. She had been going to a chiropractor for nine months, and each time she would be in agony for days. But she kept going back on the assumption that it was doing some good, until eventually she just could not take any more. She was considering trying acupuncture, but after talking to me decided to give healing a try first.

She sat on our stool in our front room while I proceeded to give healing. Working with my hands at a slight distance from her back, I noticed that she kept shifting her position. I thought it must be very painful for her to sit like this, so after twenty minutes I decided to stop. I went around to the front and saw that she had her eyes closed and an expression on her face not of pain, but of pleasure. So I carried on and worked for another twenty minutes. She later told me that it felt as if muscles in her back were gently unknotting, as a consequence of which she had to keep adjusting her balance. She was amazed at the benefit she received through healing when I hadn't even touched her! She came several more times, improving each time.

After this she used to come to us now and then, and she found that after each session she ached for days before getting better, so she would plan her visits so she had time the following day or two to do very little. The overall effect of these visits was very positive however, and she now has little trouble walking or gardening. She never did go for acupuncture.

Also as a consequence of the healing, she has become very interested in the spiritual side of the paranormal and I have managed to help her get rid of an unseen, but very real, problem presence she called Darth Vader that had plagued her since childhood, and made her afraid of the dark. Walking home from work one day, knowing that 'Darth Vader' would be there waiting for her, she decided to try sending Light to her home. She says she felt his surprise as he was suddenly whooshed away! She has positively blossomed, and is now helping other people to understand some of the mysteries of life. A real success story!

Some time after this another colleague benefited from my healing. She had asked Keith and me to visit her home to talk with her eight year old daughter about the paranormal phenomena she was experiencing. As Keith talked with her daughter, I sat and talked with my colleague, who was a born worrier, and had been told by her doctor that she had fibroids, and who had booked her in for a scan to confirm this. I felt that this problem had something to do with the negativity that surrounded her, so I did my best to cut the cords that still bound her to her ex-husband, and any others there might be, before I gave her healing. Two weeks later she had her scan – and much to the surprise of her doctor, it was clear!

Not everyone benefits. We once had a man come for healing and never return. He had a dream that night that his head had turned into an onion and blamed us (and the healing) for that! More likely it was his own fears surfacing.

However, the majority of patients do find some benefit from healing, although not necessarily at the first session, and those few who don't have lost only a bit of time and effort, for healing has no adverse side effects when practised responsibly (except sometimes temporarily as noted above). Some can feel heat, cold or tingling, which shows that something is happening, but many feel nothing except relaxed – either way the healing can still work.

Of course, if the cause of the problem is not dealt with no amount of healing will be of permanent benefit, so if the cause is on-going - diet or life-style related for instance - then it is up to the patient to take responsibility for improving their own health.

I remember reading that Harry Edwards, who was one of this country's most well known and respected healers and took meticulous notes, had worked out that of all the people who came for healing 80% benefited, of which 20% were cured, leaving just 20% who received no measurable benefit. Bear in mind that the majority of his patients were those who could get no further help from the medical profession, suffering either from a terminal illness or with something they would 'have to learn to live with'. Also bear in mind that no-one can measure the possible benefit which healing may have been to those facing their last days.

Some people use crystals in their healing work, and crystal healing is becoming increasingly popular. Our introduction to crystals took place many years ago now. I remember going to a 'Psychic & Mystics Fair', as they used to be called - now they are called 'Mind, Body & Spirit' events. I was standing by a stall laid out with many different crystals, reading a sheet about how to cleanse crystals. I became aware that my head was beginning to feel very strange, and I realised this was because of the combined power of all those crystals! So I asked to take the sheet further away to read it – having done so the feeling eased. This was really my first introduction to their energies.

Quite some time later we visited the caves at Cheddar. As we were walking around I spotted an area of crystals exposed in the rock – about the size of my hand. I put my hand on it to feel the power and withdrew it almost at once as the energy shot through me and almost blew my head off! It was after all, attached to an enormous amount of rock.

When you buy crystals you should always tune into their energies and choose those that harmonize with you. Remember to always cleanse them and re-tune them to your own energies and purposes.

We once gave healing to a man from Wiltshire who ran a stall selling crystals. He then progressed to a shop, where he hired an assistant. He rang us up some time later, most upset and worried as he had discovered that this assistant had programmed all of the crystals in his shop for dark purposes.

He had closed his shop and removed them all to his garage where he was at a loss as to how to deal with them. It represented a considerable outlay on his part, but he could not, in all conscience, sell them now.

He came to our house, bringing with him just one of them, a large smoky quartz, as an example. We didn't touch it, and he set it down on the carpet in our front room, about three feet away from us. As we tuned into the energies, I was aware of several lime green upright wiggly 'worms', about six inches high, coming out of it and heading towards me, but as they came they sank deeper and deeper into the carpet, as the energies in the room were too strong for them.

He left that crystal with us and we thoroughly cleansed it with salt water and sunshine, keeping it well away from all our other crystals in the meantime. We never heard what happened with the rest of them, as a garage-full was rather too much for us to deal with.

So do be careful when buying crystals!

In 2008 I experienced crystal healing for myself when I had a treatment from our friend George. I lay on his couch at a Healing Event in Weston-super-Mare as he checked first that I was laying straight, then put different coloured cloths on or by my main chakras, on which he placed various crystals (the cloths hold them better and make them easier to pick up again, especially important from a lady). He had already laid many crystals in grids underneath the couch. He worked around me for about twenty minutes, after which time I felt as if I was floating. When I got off the couch, I had to go and sit quietly for the next hour to gain maximum benefit. It felt great!

Keith experienced George's crystal healing the following month. As he lay on the couch with George working over his chakras, as in the photo below, Keith was pleasantly surprised to find his third eye opened and he saw a column of light ascending. With brief gaps in between, he saw five or six similar columns of different colours, possibly as George was working on the various chakras. On one occasion at the top of a column of white light, he saw a circle of angel-like beings. This is something he will never forget.

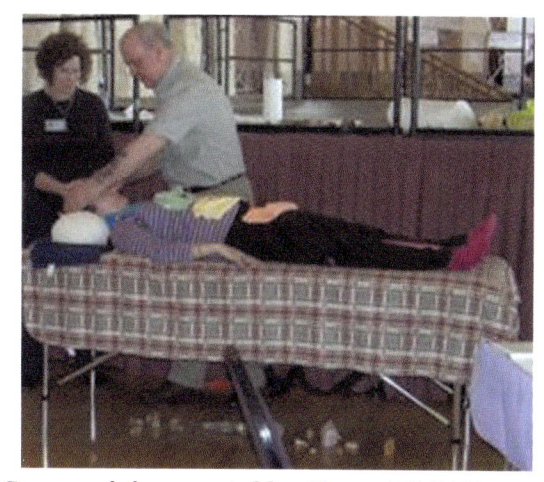

George giving crystal healing at W-S-M, 2008

From the photo at the start of this chapter, you will have realised that I work on a healing stall at various events. This is the work that Keith really wanted to do ever since he saw Dennis Fare and Edward Lester offering healing at the roadside in Burrington Combe, back in the 1970s.

We began in about 1990 by taking a stall to small local events in our old blue frame tent until, at the Village Fayre on Hanham Common in May 2002, the wind blew a window in our tent that wasn't meant to be there, as well as bending some of the poles. That day we had rain, wind, sunshine, fog and even hail. But I remember a man standing and staring at our tent with its banner. I went and spoke to him and he said he was just astonished to see us there – he said he never thought he'd see the day when such a thing would happen – he was the son of Nellie Toye, a very well known and respected local medium and healer, whom we had known well when she was in her eighties, and who had been most encouraging towards us. Also, that day was memorable for the elderly lady who had some healing from Keith for her ankle, never having had any healing before. She walked away from the tent, then turned and walked back with a big smile on her face, saying she wasn't limping any more!

We then bought a larger white marquee and continued to go to all sorts of events with it, under the banner of the Bristol and District Association of Healers (BDAH - www.bdah.btck.co.uk) whose President Dennis Fare (later Patron) and his wife Doreen always supported us and often came with us to these events. Dennis passed away in July 2011, aged 86, after a lifetime of promoting healing. We went to events that had never before had healing of any kind offered, like the Castle Combe Steam and Vintage Fair; the Cat Show; the Oldland Horticultural Show and Village Fayre; Bristol Volkfest; Bristol Vegan Fayres – as well as to events designed to publicise healing such as Bill Harrison's Healing Weekends, and various Mind, Body & Spirit ones.

Not all stalls paid their way, but we took enough overall to cover our expenses. It took three years to recoup the cost of the marquee from the donations. The point, though, was not to make money but to introduce members of the public to healing and bring it out into the open, which it now is.

We tried to ensure that those who had healing always left knowing where they could get more in their own locality.

We have given up some events now, as there are others offering complementary therapies, which was never the case before, and because now it is much more in the public eye it is no longer so necessary – and of course, we're all getting older.

One event stands out even though we only went once. It was a two-day military vehicle event at Berkeley Castle, Gloucestershire. Keith and I went the day before to put up the marquee (it was the first time we had used it), and as Keith was securing it I wandered around to look at the old vehicles that were there. At an old Red Cross army vehicle that would have been used in World War Two, I was aware of some of the previous occupants from that time still around it. Of course, I tuned into them and helped them to cross over.

The following day when other healers from BDAH arrived, they couldn't believe what Keith had asked them to come to! The atmosphere was so heavy, and charged with lower vibrations! A lot of the visitors that day were dressed in old military uniforms, and a stall near us selling children's toys was also selling, for adults, military books and, horrifyingly, guns! Nonetheless we had eleven people who had healing that day, and many more that we talked to. On that first day our friend Davey twice walked around the whole site sending out Light.

The only laughter we heard that day was coming from our stall and the one next to us, which was manned by a very helpful and cheery man selling Jeep parts, who had helped us erect our marquee on the Friday and had even given us two very useful old mail sacks to keep the canvases in, and a whole load of 'bobbles' to attach them to the poles.

The second day the atmosphere was much lighter, and there were many more children around and fewer 'posers'. The second day we gave healing to 24 people. We knew we had done what was needed and so never went again.

One year at the Castle Combe Steam and Vintage Fair a lady came up to the stall, pointed at Doreen, and said accusingly, "You're to blame!" "Okay", said Doreen, "but what did I do?" The lady said, "Last year you dragged me into the tent and gave me healing, and now I can't get enough of it! I love it!"

Doreen & Keith at Castle Combe Steam and Vintage Fair, 2006

You may have realised from the above account of the venues we do healing at that, unlike many healers, we do not need peace and quiet in order to work. Having developed our gifts at the same time as raising two lively children it was never going to be so, and it just isn't us! We have deliberately trained ourselves to give healing in any circumstances, so that background noise and conversations don't bother us in the least, indeed we often join in with the conversations, even whilst the healing is flowing through us to someone else. Some healers may disapprove, but it certainly helps ease any tension anyone may feel and the relaxed, informal atmosphere created is very much appreciated by those who come.

Keith at our Fishponds Drop-in Healing Clinic

I had been running a monthly meditation/development group at The Elemental Sanctuary since October 2005, and in June 2006 we started a weekly Drop-in Healing Clinic there.

This was held in a large square soundproof room at the back of an old Victorian semi-detached house on the main road through Fishponds to which therapy rooms had been added at the back. We would not have been able to do this if it had not been for the owner's generosity in letting us use the room for no set fee, just a share of the donations, as we would not have been able to cover a commercial rent.

The healing was given in front of everyone in the room, although we did have access to other rooms if someone wished for more privacy. It developed a very nice friendly atmosphere, where the patients quickly become friends – not just with us, but with each other too. We had one man who caught two buses to come, and yet sometimes had no hands-on healing, just sitting there with us for an hour or so losing himself in the gentle music, and then going home quite happily, having received his healing from the energies in the room itself. Several patients stayed long after they had had their healing – just because they loved it there, sometimes all four hours. Often it seemed like a social occasion where friends met once a week, and, instead of having coffee, they had healing in between their conversations. We built up a regular clientele who loved to come, as much for the lovely friendly atmosphere as for the hands-on healing.

In July 2008, whilst attending the Remembrance Ceremony for Bill Harrison, where his collections of books, CDs etc. were being sold, I was inspired to buy his Neil H CD *'Resonation of Angels'*. This was recorded at the end of an angel workshop in Cornwall where the participants had made several paintings of various archangels. Neil had, in turn, set one of the paintings in front of him and then recorded the music he was inspired to play - in all he did this for seven archangel paintings.

When it was played at the Drop-in Healing Clinic the following Thursday Mairi, who had intended to walk home, stayed until the end – simply because of the music. Our long-time friend Charlie also loved it.

The following week we played it again. Towards the end of the session, about 5.20, only Keith, myself, Mairi and our student healer Fliss were there. I was showing Fliss photos of our 40th anniversary cruise, and Keith was giving Mairi some extra healing as her neck still hurt. Mairi interrupted Fliss and me to ask Fliss if she could see an angel by her, as Keith had sensed that there was one present. Fliss confirmed this saying that the angel was standing parallel to Keith in the corner. I too tuned in. I commented that I sensed that the angel was really tall. I was also aware of a portion of his wings, which were a soft gold colour in a pattern on a background of white, and edged with a very thin line of black. I asked Fliss if his shoulders were level with the ceiling, which she confirmed, making him about 10 or 11 feet tall - a little later I sensed him shrinking. He shrank until he was the same height as Keith. Fliss confirmed all of this. Unlike her, none of this could I see, only sense.

He then drew very near to Keith, who felt it was the angel corresponding to the music that was playing, which proved to be Archangel Jophiel. Shortly thereafter Jophiel began to talk through Keith, and gently corrected my pronunciation from **J**ophiel to **Y**ophiel. He went on to say that Archangel Michael had asked him to oversee our clinic and us. He, Jophiel, had been around us for some time, but the music had enabled the archangels named to draw much closer. He also said when we return in September we would find an improvement in the atmosphere, and our healing would be more powerful; and that they want the clinic to continue so they will continue to give help to Carole (the owner of the premises, who has considered selling). He said we will find that some of our current patients will no longer need to come, and that we will be surprised at some of the new patients we will get. When I commented that if we get more patients we will need more help, he said we already have a good team of three. We have since had another two healers join our team. He also confirmed to Keith that Archangel Raphael had been working with him not only on Mairi but also earlier on another patient.

During 2008, in 45 sessions, we treated a total of 61 individuals, including 4 children, plus one dog, giving a total of 386 healing treatments. (The following year the total number of treatments went up to 546). In addition, we had a student healer training with us. We are also fortunate in that we can call on other Bristol District Association of Healers members to cover for us if we are away, or indeed, ill (which seldom happens, but it is good to have that support).

Sometimes the atmosphere was almost like a party, with much banter and laughter. In January 2009 one patient/new friend brought another friend along. This man had a lovely smile that lit up his face – beautiful white teeth against his black skin, and eyes that shone, a truly lovely personality. As I talked with him, I discovered he suffered with a bad back.

Now, over the years our healing styles have changed, maybe as the healing has got more powerful, or maybe as we have gained more experience. Either way Keith now works mainly on the head, neck, shoulders and spine, and therefore specialises in back problems – of which there are many. So I called Keith over and asked this man, Carlton, to tell Keith what the problem was. He started by saying he had a bad back, at which Keith's eyes, and indeed, whole face, lit up, and he exclaimed gleefully, "Oh good!". I was walking away, but I turned and said to him in mock horror, "You can't say that! You're supposed to be a healer, and so should be showing sympathy and empathy, not saying "Oh good" when someone tells you they have a bad back!" By which time everyone was laughing, as they all knew he hadn't meant it like that - he just likes the challenge. Carlton took it very well, laughing along with everyone else as Keith stood looking a bit embarrassed but unabashed, and he came back for more for many weeks thereafter - his presence, with his lovely smile, lighting up the room.

We all had a good laugh - even the following week when we related the incident to those who had not been there. A couple of weeks later Archangel Michael, speaking through Keith at home, commented that they too had all enjoyed the laugh, and that the incident had been recorded on the Akashic record, where, presumably, others might enjoy it too. Pity it wasn't recorded on film, as it would have made a brilliant comedy sketch.

As for me, I have nearly always worked with my hands slightly away from the body, because I can then be more aware of the slightest feelings in my fingers as to when and where the healing is needed most. I also feel the patient can relax more if they are not aware of where the hands of the healer are until we give their shoulders a little squeeze at the end and say "Bless you". There are some people who like to feel hands upon them, and some occasions when I feel inspired to do so.

I usually start my healing at the head, then progress down the back. I then move to the side of the patient and hold my hands at back and front of each chakra in turn. Then I move my hands over each arm and leg, then over the front of the person, before returning to stand behind the patient, where I finish by sealing the healing within the aura. How long I stay at each point, and where exactly my hands go, is dictated by the feelings I get both through my hands and my intuition.

Always after receiving healing we recommend that people drink lots of water, and we always have it available. We also make sure that no-one leaves without being properly grounded, as if they are still too relaxed or have their heads in the clouds they can be a danger to themselves and others.

My healing is in the process of changing again now since I have been approved as a practitioner of crystal healing and chakra balancing.

Once Carlton brought a friend of his who had only just flown in from New York. I gave him healing and I haven't seen him since, but Carlton later reported that he was delighted with the healing as the pain in his shoulder had disappeared and had only returned when he got back to New York a fortnight later!

In April 2009, at our Drop-in Healing Clinic, Keith gave healing to Pauline, a therapist, who had injured her right leg the previous Monday whilst staying in a friend's caravan. She had been encouraging an elderly Alsatian dog to come out of the caravan and had stepped backwards out of the door, but had missed the step and ended up thwacking the front of her leg against the underside of the caravan. She felt at the time that she had "done some damage there'" A large bruise had come up, but it didn't subside; a lump came up over the bone, and it was very painful. By the Friday a distinct red line had appeared around the leg several inches below the knee, and was moving up the leg by the hour. She was worried enough to take herself to the hospital (the first time in at least 20 years), but the nurse there had taken a brief look, told her it was just a bruise and told her to go home - which she did. But she felt it was more than that, she felt a bone had chipped, and she was angry at having been turned away without being listened to, and without even being seen by a doctor. So she asked us what we felt.

I held my right hand above the injury. Soon I felt a coolness coming from my hand, which she was also aware of. I was given a picture in my mind of a bone that had diagonally split apart jaggedly. I then held my other hand a little away from the underside of the leg, allowing the energies to flow between my two hands. After a while Pauline drew in a short sharp breath of pain, as she felt something move inside her leg. This happened several more times, but she was happy for me to continue as she knew something was being put right. At no time did my hands touch her leg.

After a while I felt a sense of relief from the leg, as if the bones had been put back where they belonged – a feeling that she confirmed. But the healing and the intermittent pain continued as the surrounding tissues had also to be put right. She said she has a high threshold of pain, but after a while this pain was so intense and accumulative, that she began to feel sick and light-headed. When eventually I felt able to withdraw my hands I went looking for something for her to be sick in, unsuccessfully, so she limped her way to the toilet, but by the time she got there it had passed, although it still took her some time to recover from what had been a very painful and unexpected experience. By the time we parted at about 6.20 the bruising had noticeably reduced, as had the lump.

A totally unexpected experience for all of us, and a dramatic example of psychic surgery.

After five years of our Drop-in Healing Clinic at The Elemental Sanctuary we are now (Sept 2011) seeking new premises, or maybe we will enter a new phase of our life, as the room we used has become unavailable due to a change of use.

In those five years we have been privileged to help many people and some animals, and have also made many friends along the way.

I will close this chapter with the following account by a patient of ours, Mairi, who has become one of those friends. You may remember her from earlier when I was telling you about her greyhound Rhia in the chapter on animals.

A Personal Account of the Benefits of Healing

"I first met my friends Helen & Keith Bevan in September [2006], *when they very kindly came to my home in Staple Hill, Bristol, in order to give me healing for back problems and depression.*

I had a long history of problems in this area from childhood which had culminated in July, when I had undergone neurosurgery to remove bone spurs from my spinal cord. I was also suffering from severe arthritis in the neck, which was quite painful and causing me to feel low, both mentally and physically.

Over many years, I had tried several other treatments to alleviate my symptoms including osteopathy, chiropractic, physiotherapy and even hot wax therapy, unfortunately none of these had proved to have any real lasting beneficial effect. As a result of my illness, I had been unable to do any paid work for about 15 years and had to use a V pillow to support my back almost all the time, even when I went out socially or to attend Helen's meditation group at Fishpond's Elemental Sanctuary, which was rather inconvenient and cumbersome to say the least! I am now able to sit without support and thankfully have regained much of my lost mobility.

Helen and Keith would come regularly every Friday morning and I would receive Healing from Keith who is particularly gifted in helping people suffering from back problems, with many different root causes. Slowly and surely over the months my problems gradually reduced and my spinal flexibility increased. Keith had warned me at the outset that any improvements shown would be gradual, as otherwise the problems would recur over time and no sustained improvement would be likely to be made.

As I progressed over time, I was able to accompany Helen & Keith to Fishpond's Elemental Sanctuary nearby on Thursday afternoons to help prepare the Healing room there: setting out chairs and laying out the leaflets, books, newsletters etc. offered to clients by the Bevans. I was also able to benefit from regular weekly treatments from Keith and, latterly, from Helen too.

After about a year I was able to walk back home from the Sanctuary, which is about 1½ miles door to door. There is absolutely no way I could have achieved this without Healing and several times recently I've walked there <u>and</u> back on a pleasant day, covering around 3 miles on the round trip. This is a massive achievement for me, as for many years I wouldn't have been capable of making the journey one way, far less both, which is absolute proof to me that healing <u>works</u>!

I would strongly advise anyone with a chronic condition such as back problems to give Healing a chance, as they have nothing whatsoever to lose and quite possibly a great deal to gain from this particular form of Spiritual treatment."

Mairi McGonigill Sept 2008

She has since gone from strength to strength, mainly because she has taken control of her life and is very good at following our advice. She now meditates every day, and has worked very hard on her emotional issues from this life and past lives.

When we picked her up in February 2010 we watched as she came round the corner, realised we were waiting for her, and broke into a trot! She would never have been able to do that only 18 months previously.

A year later Mairi seldom comes for healing as she enjoys many trips out on Thursdays with a friend who delivers parcels around the South-West. She is so grateful for the ability now to get out and about.

Sacred Spaces

Glastonbury Tor

As I was growing up, my Dad used to take us to a lot of parish churches, not because he was a religious man, he wasn't (spiritual, yes, but not particularly religious) but because he was interested in the architecture. So I grew up knowing the different feeling that you get in these old churches, some more than others. Later I worked in libraries where the atmosphere again was different to normal, although not in the same way. (This is not so noticeable these days as the public libraries have tried to make themselves more user-friendly). I well remember the times I used the old St. George Library as a child – having to creep about trying not to make the slightest noise, even with squeaky shoes, for fear of people glaring at me; having to stay in the children's section of this huge, towering, building, with its tall bookcases; and the total and unnatural hush that was about the place.

Many people are sensitive to these kinds of atmosphere and can feel the welcome or otherwise of a building the moment they enter, even if it is empty at the time. A lot of people have commented on how welcoming and warm our home is, even though it is usually in quite a mess.

Maybe these early years helped me to develop these senses more than most. Sometimes I will enter certain churches or other buildings and be overwhelmed by the difference in the feel of the place, so much so that sometimes it stops me in my tracks. I often feel this when I am the first one to arrive at our Drop-in Healing Clinic - it feels holy, as if it has already been prepared for use. However, this is not reserved just for the inside of buildings. It can also happen out in the open at places like Stonehenge, or in cemeteries, or totally out of the blue as in the case I related earlier, in the chapter on residual energies, as I walked near my home.

In 1984 I accompanied the school children when they had a trip to the prehistoric site of Avebury from the primary school, as they were short of a female 'responsible adult' on the coaches. When they got there I was no longer needed to supervise so I strolled off on my own. It was a drizzly day so there were few people about.

I walked slowly down the centre of the Avenue of standing stones trying to tune in to the time when this was being used – I sensed a crowd of people in festival mood coming the other way (towards the stone circle). Amongst them were people in white robes with different coloured corded belts who seemed to me to be initiates of varying degrees. They would be approached by people who obviously wanted their help and who they would direct to stand between particular pairs of stones while the crowd flowed past them.

I felt the stones alternated both down the lines and across with what we might call masculine and feminine energies. I tried to tune in to a pair that might help me, and felt the stones awakening from their slumber. Having identified a particular pair that might help me, I stood equi-distant between them for a while. After receiving their help I felt I should leave something as a thank-you – but what? Money seemed inappropriate and the only thing I had on me that might do was a crystal pendant I was wearing. I took that off and laid it at the base of one of the stones, but as I turned to leave I felt that I could retrieve it as being prepared to leave it was enough. I felt this was the way these stones had been used a few times a year, at particular and well-known festivals.

I also tuned in within the circle at a line of seven stones flanked by two pairs of stones and opposite the site of the obelisk (now a concrete pillar). I felt the pairs of flanking stones were there to act as a boundary and to hold the energies within the space, and the obelisk would have had a large clear crystal placed upon it at certain times. When the sun shone it would split the rays like a prism and each of the seven stones represented a different one of those colours. The people in need would be directed to one of those stones to obtain its healing power.

When my children were a little older I remember visiting the stone circles at Stanton Drew. One of the large stones was sharply angled and very knobbly yet my son, then aged about 12 or 13, had climbed up on it and laid down. It looked most uncomfortable yet he said he felt he could go to sleep there – so I said it must have been the dreaming stone.

On another visit later with Keith I sensed that one of the stones would have been the main stone, so I respectfully asked its permission to put some crystals on it to cleanse them and absorb some of its power. As I stood in front of it in sacred mode, I telepathically received a series of dots as if they were words. It seemed I was being asked for a responding code in order to gain access to something beyond. I was unable to as no dots came into my mind, nor any other response.

On my birthday in March 1984 we went for the first time to the White Eagle Lodge at Liss, Hampshire. I had recently become a member as I loved the simplicity of White Eagle's teachings – easy to understand yet hard to live up to. [White Eagle is the name of the very much respected spirit guide of the late Grace Cooke]. The temple at Liss is on a hill and was designed by White Eagle and his band of helpers themselves. It is tucked away amidst lovely grounds with the original house nearby. The temple complex is all white with a golden sun-disc emblazoned across the front, representing the soul's ability to fly, so it is a remarkable sight as you first approach it; the temple itself is circular. Inside the atmosphere is beautiful. The circular dome has at its centre a round glass window with the symbol of the rose on the cross within it. Above the altar hangs a large 3D crystal star, with the rows of seats arranged in semi-circular fashion in front of it. Whilst there I asked where was the nearest group to me and was amazed to be told it was actually in my own village! I have been going there, on and off, ever since.

One year we took a group of people to the Easter service at Liss, which was fantastic – one of our group said he could hear a choir of angels singing along with us.

I would certainly recommend a visit if it is at all possible.

There are now two other such temples, at Maleny, near Brisbane, Australia and at Montgomery, Texas, America.

When I take services I often take my reading from White Eagle's books, as does Keith.

Many years ago when were driving past Glastonbury we linked in with the Tor and I felt that the Guardian of the Tor was in trouble. Glastonbury is a magical place but it is a magnet for both those on the path of Light and those on the opposite path. I felt the forces of Darkness had managed to imprison the Guardian of the Tor in some kind of vortex of energy, so we found a place to stop underneath the Tor and both sent out our prayers for the Guardian to be helped. After a little while we felt this had been achieved and he was free once more. After that we always sent out our thoughts whenever we were in the vicinity, and occasionally felt we needed to send extra energy his way.

Another time we were in the Chalice Gardens when we linked in, and that time we felt the Guardian was under attack again, so we helped out.

One day when we had climbed the Tor, we stopped about half way down and sent out our thoughts over the whole surrounding area. I linked in with Wearyall Hill and 'saw' (in my mind's eye) a fountain of light come up out of the hill and spread all over the surrounding countryside.

We first met Adam Yellow Bird DeArmon at the July 2004 Healing Event at Bill Harrison's, where I saw him and his wife Carmen perform a lengthy Native American ceremony to bless a marriage. The following weekend he was holding an Earth Healing Ceremony in the Glastonbury Healing Centre.

We arranged to take Dave Pearse and meet our friends Greta and Steve down there with the intention of climbing the Tor and having a picnic there before the ceremony. We arrived in the designated car-park just after 11 a.m. Greta and Steve had not arrived by 11.30, nor could we reach them by mobile phone, so we went off on our own. Firstly we booked in for the ceremony then set off along the road towards the Tor – but it was raining and Dave's sandals were slipping on the wet paving stones. He went barefoot, but given that we only had less than two hours, and it was not suitable weather for a picnic, I tried to think of somewhere else to go. I noticed a sign across the road that said "St Mary Magdalene's Chapel and Almshouses", so we went there. Despite many visits to Glastonbury over the years we did not know this place existed. It was a delightfully quiet oasis, where we ate our picnic on a wooden bench under the protection of an archway.

Afterwards I went alone into the chapel and sat awhile in the peace and quiet. Later the two men joined me and Keith said a prayer aloud. During this he was taken over by a spirit who welcomed us to this church, for although it was a Christian church he said all people were welcome who came in peace and love, as we did. He told us our other two friends were now nearby (and so it turned out) and that he was the Guardian of this place, who was in contact with our own guides and also with the Guardian of the Tor, who was grateful for the help we had given him previously. It appears that the Guardianship changes from time to time and it would soon be changing again. *A wonderful, and totally unexpected, experience!*

At the Glastonbury Healing Centre, after watching a video about Earth Dance, about 20 of us gathered downstairs whilst Adam drew a six-pointed star in a circle on the floor with cornmeal and did a short ceremony to cleanse the stargate/vortex there and protect it from harmful use. We then all sat upstairs in a circle while Adam laid out an altar on the floor. I provided a fan to symbolise the wind element, and also put my new animal oracle cards down to have them blessed and to symbolise the animals and our knowledge of them. Keith put down his Native American pendant that our daughter had given him: Dave put a branch of an apple tree: Greta put healing herbs. During the ensuing ceremony Adam used my cards, and two dragon cards were chosen, plus the hind, symbolising the ley lines and the mystical connection to the other world. Dave presented Adam with the apple branch, which he seemed pleased with and will fashion into a walking stick. We all thoroughly enjoyed the day, with its new experiences and its synchronicities.

The following Thursday, 22nd July 2004, we met up with Adam Yellow Bird again, this time at Avebury. We again took Dave Pearse, though Greta and Steve were unable to come.
About a dozen of us took part in an earth ceremony not far from the obelisk – a spot picked out by Adam, and confirmed by Dave who dowsed with a borrowed pendulum. At each of the directions Adam placed stakes with different coloured ribbons on, about 20 paces from the centre, and then four of us took turns to link each stake with a thin line of cornflour. At the centre he built an altar, with fire in a small flower pot, a stake with his Earth Dance emblem and coloured ribbons on, and various other bits. I put down a pen (for communication), then Keith put down his silver Native American pendant and his mobile phone, Dave put in two black feathers he had collected. Other people put a variety of crystals, a bottle of water, a rattle ...

He then asked an older lady and gentleman to lead us, her with a smoking sage brush and him shaking the rattle, away from the altar towards the large pair of stones, where we stopped to connect to them. They then led us back to the altar while Adam banged his drum and sang. When we reached the circle we walked around it in a clockwise direction a few times, led by Carmen as Adam stood outside the circle drumming and singing, then we walked in the other direction. We then moved as one into the middle, where we slowly circled, then out again. A most unusual and interesting experience for us!

On occasions we have been called to help people who live on ley lines. One such case was near Cheddar where we felt the problems in the house were caused by the fact that one of the two ley lines, that crossed as they ran through her home, was blocked. We cleared it.

This reminds me of the time many years ago when we were visiting ancient sites in and around Oxfordshire, including the Rollwright Stones, and the Whispering Knights. We had taken a packed lunch and stopped to eat it at the side of a quiet road. Afterwards we sat quietly sending out our thoughts to the surrounding area. We linked in with ley lines that were running nearby and sent our thoughts along them sending the Light. We were astonished to feel that this light was being carried right down the line to St Michael's Mount, then under the English Channel to Mont St Michel on the other side!

We felt we had helped revitalise a rather sluggish ley line.

Past Lives

Me in 2002

I didn't grow up believing in re-incarnation, but have come to accept it through a mixture of logic and my own experiences. Believing as I do in a superior power that we generally call God, and also in the survival of the spirit after death it just did not seem right that there should only be one life. How can anyone learn all the lessons that are needed if they only have one life? Sometimes a very short one. It made much more sense to me that there should be multiple lives in multiple circumstances. I compare it to our education system – everyone gets a basic education, and most progress much further. Later some specialise, and then many go on to University or college, a few progressing even further. In a similar way each life will add to the store of knowledge but not just academically or practically but to a much broader degree. There are many lessons to be learnt, and often the individual has to repeat certain experiences many times until they finally learn the lesson.

I do not believe that we are forced to return but choose when and where to do so in order to progress. Also that we choose which lessons we want to have a go at, and so also choose the circumstances we will find ourselves in. It is then the job of each person's guide and guardian angel to help provide the opportunities necessary.

Over the years I have remembered snippets of many of my past lives. Invariably they are connected with someone I know now or something I am going through at the time. They have helped explain why things are as they are and have on occasions helped me to decide what to do.

For instance, whilst we were active in the Hillfields' church in the late 1970s & early 1980s we were friendly with a young man, about 23 years old, who was also friendly with the lady whose house we were later asked to clear by her estranged husband.

At that time we knew that she was involved in some dubious psychic practices, which we had to counter as best we could. In other words we were engaged in psychic battle. As with any battle you do not want to let your opponent know what you are doing or planning to do. This young man knew there was something going on and wanted to know what. For some reason I was reluctant to tell him and spent some time pondering whether to or not. Eventually my memory opened up to the last time I had been a man.

The year was 1941. I was a Dutchman of about 30 years of age, operating in France in the early days of the Resistance. I 'saw' myself leading a small group down from a grey stone bridge on a dusty road to the railway line below. We walked some way along the track and set explosives to sabotage the line. The trees alongside were in summer foliage. My memory fast forwarded to a clear autumn evening. I was at a village crossroads, a square with a stone monument at its centre. The streets were cobbled, the houses built of grey stone, and the scene was lit by bright moonlight. I was pressed against a stone wall in the shadows, having just seen my best friend Henri gunned down by the Germans, who had obviously been waiting for us. I tried to escape over the back gardens but I knew I had not succeeded. It appeared that we had been betrayed by the youngest member of our cell, who was very proud to be in the Resistance and had been unable to resist bragging to his girlfriend, who, being cleverer than him, had used the information to gain some advantage for her and her mother.

No prizes for guessing that that young man was the same soul as the one I felt reluctant to trust this time round!

The same young man got on extremely well with our daughter, who was about eight at that time. It transpired that a few hundred years ago she was my sister and he was her young man. I remembered the three of us strolling over some very pleasant undulating green countryside.

A little later I began to do some work for a rather pleasant man a few years younger than me. He would pop in regularly to see how things were going. He never criticised me and was obviously appreciative of the work I was doing. However, I found myself getting increasingly anxious every time he was due – I became afraid of his moods and desperately wanted to please him. This was not like me – I don't much care what people think of me – I follow the axiom 'to thine own self be true'. Moreover he had never shown me any evidence of moodiness. Yet this feeling was getting more and more pronounced and so I spent quite a bit of time trying to understand why.

Then one day, my past life memory opened up and showed me a scene high up in the mountains on a large grassy plateau. I felt it was somewhat to the north-west of where I live now, at a time when the weather hereabouts was much warmer and sunnier than it is these days, somewhere between 2,000 and 10,000 years ago. And in a land that was not Britain as we know it now.

I was the daughter of the chief of one tribe and this man was the son of a chief of another tribe. We were about the same age – 17 or 18 – and we were getting married for the sake of the tribes, who were gathered below us en masse to witness the event. We had never met before, and although we accepted that our fathers had the right to marry us like this, as we got to the last part of the ceremony where we turned to each other with arms outstretched (my palms up, his palms down and covering mine) we looked deep into each others eyes to see if we might find personal happiness too. I believe we did.

This made me realise that my problem stemmed from a past life - not that one though.
In 2003 I visited Carreck Castle in mid Wales and felt this was the area referred to above, though it would have looked very different topographically then.

Some time later, when the same problem was still troubling me, I had another memory. This time the year was 1888 and I was the youngest of three daughters of a Judge Walters living in a small but fashionable provincial town, such as Bath might have been, or Cheltenham or York. I had fallen madly in love with a dashing junior army officer, about six years older than my tender 18 years. I used to sneak out of a little used pointed door in the surrounding tall grey stone wall of our estate to meet him. My father was against the match but I managed to persuade him and so we married and I moved from the country home of my father to a town house.

This was at a time when the only sex education genteel young ladies received was an embarrassed 'lie back and think of England' from their mothers – and I had not even had that! However, my new husband was gentle and patient with me and taught me to enjoy that side of marriage. I bore him three healthy sons over the next six years and was deliriously happy. Each time I was pregnant he would cease visiting my bed until six months after the birth. I missed him, but I realised he did it out of concern for me. The last pregnancy was a difficult one and I almost lost my life. After six months he did not come back to my bed and I supposed this to be because of the difficult time I had had – he must be allowing longer out of respect for me.

Time passed and he still did not come back, so I ventured to say something about missing him (such things were not spoken of in those days). He patted me kindly on the head and said "Yes, dear", but still he did not come back. I began to think there must be another reason, so I took a good look at myself and realised I had put on some weight and my clothes were out-of-date... So I took myself in hand, working hard at getting my figure back and looking more as befitted the wife of a captain (to which office he had by then been promoted). He was obviously pleased I had gone to so much trouble – but he still did not come back. What else could it be? I took to surreptitiously watching him and discovered that he went with, what at that time were called, 'scarlet women'.

This came as quite a shock to me because although a married woman with three sons I was still an innocent. But I loved him so much that I would have done anything for him, so if that was what he liked than I would try to provide it for him. I secretly watched these scarlet women carefully and studied how they dressed, how they made-up, how they moved, and how they behaved, all quite different from my class of lady. I acquired all the necessary requisites and practised in the privacy of my own room, until I was confident I had got it right. Then one evening when our sons were in bed and the servants gone I greeted him at the door as he came in, fully expecting him to be pleased at how much effort I had made to please him. Instead he was furious and told me to get that muck off my face, and out of those clothes immediately and to never do such a thing again. I was heartbroken. What was it that he wanted? It appeared he wanted nothing from me except to be a good mother to his children and a good hostess when we entertained or went anywhere. He didn't _love me_! It became clear to me that he could not _ever_ have loved me, and must have married me only for the status, and the help my father could give him.

Divorce in those days was out of the question, so I drew on my pride and performed the role of wife and mother to the best of my ability, so well in fact that everyone thought we were the ideal couple. Indeed he seemed happy enough, but to me our marriage was just an empty shell, and I frequently used to cry myself to sleep.

After the youngest of our children was about 14 years old, and therefore of an age when he didn't need his mother so much, I looked ahead to the remainder of my life and decided I couldn't face maybe another 20 years of this sham marriage, so I left a note explaining why and just took off. I went to London and lost myself amongst the down-and-outs alongside the Thames. Eventually, and after not too long as I really didn't care, I died of a broken heart and was buried, unknown, in a pauper's grave.

Subsequent to this surfacing of a memory, I discovered that my husband had gone frantic – he really had no idea I was so unhappy, thinking that he did not love me. In fact he loved me very much, and because of this had behaved in the way he'd been taught to behave with well-bred women. He thought I had allowed him to sleep with me firstly from a desire to procreate and secondly out of wifely duty.

He had gone with scarlet women to spare me the need to satisfy his animal desires. He thought that was the right thing to do. And my attempts to lure him back to the marital bed he assumed had been made from a keen sense of duty. He had searched everywhere he could think of for me, eventually being forced to give up. He then spent the remainder of his life in bitter loneliness, ostracised by society for the perceived wrong he had done me. On top of which, despite my best efforts, our sons had grown up knowing of my deep unhappiness and blaming him for that.

Keith told me at the time that in that life he had been my grandfather and much later Keith's spirit guide told me that he had been one of my sons, and now understood and so had forgiven his then father. That leaves only two that I have still to trace and persuade them to forgive.

I tried hard this time round to make it up with this man, with limited success, although I do believe there is now no karma between us, as we have each forgiven the other.
However, it has obviously left a deep scar on him as he is now afraid of commitment, which only goes to show how important it is to openly and honestly discuss things. Misunderstandings can have such profound and long-lasting effects!

Other lives I remember snippets of are:-

France. I was a young expectant mother with two young children at my side watching from the doorway of our humble country cottage as my husband went off to fight for the king with all the other young males from the area. All of them were simple peasants. I know I never saw him again in that life.
In this life he was someone I knew through Raja Yoga.

Ancient Egypt. I was the daughter of the head builder of one of the Egyptian pyramids. He was in charge of teams of priests who were positioned in groups at each corner of the structure and had to co-ordinate their efforts as they used their mental powers to raise and position great blocks of stone.
I have recently been told by a colleague that a problem I was having with my mouth and throat was due to my loyalty and vow of silence that I had made to Rameses. On researching this name, I assume this refers to Rameses the Great, an ancient Egyptian Pharaoh who was renowned for building great temples. So it may have been the same life. Having formally rescinded any such vows made at any time in my past, my problem has now resolved itself.

1641, Edinburgh. I was a young woman making my way stealthily around the narrow lanes. This was just a couple of years before the start of the English Civil War. I was part of an underground movement and didn't want to be seen. Later I was the guide to a young man disguised as a woman that I was leading through Edinburgh and out into the surrounding countryside, which I knew well, helping him escape to the North-West of Scotland. This involved laying low in outlying barns or sometimes under hedges and travelling by night, which took several days.

Eventually I remembered waving him goodbye and watching him stride out across the hills, feeling very relieved that I had got him to safety.

I 'saw' myself much later in the same life as a very old woman with a family around me working at some craft outside a stone cottage. I don't believe I ever saw that young man again, though I sometimes thought of him.

In this life, he was someone I met when he came to Bristol for a Hunt Saboteurs Association AGM and was one of seventeen who stayed overnight with us – it should only have been two, but at the AGM the rest found that their pre-arranged accommodation had fallen through and so Keith invited them to stay with us! We had four tents pitched on our small lawn! This was in 1978 and we were new to the HSA, never intending to be active as we had two young children to consider – we had read in '*Howl*' (their magazine) of the hunt violence that was frequently encountered and we didn't dare risk it. We didn't quite know what to expect, having so many strangers as guests – but we were very pleasantly surprised to find every last one of them was vegetarian. It was a really great weekend!

In another life I was a Jewess in England at a time when the practice of our religion was banned (which I hadn't realised it ever had been). I remember going down an alleyway in our town to a church where we Jews congregated and worshipped in a Christian-looking way. But behind a secret door was another large room, with dark Jacobean-looking panelling, where we celebrated our secret rites and taught our children.

I was a single young woman and in my everyday life I had fallen in love with a Gentile, who also loved me but did not know that I was a Jew. I was torn between telling him and risking losing not only him but also my freedom, or continuing to deceive him, which was making me deeply unhappy. I had decided to risk telling him and was walking with him towards the above building when events took the decision out of my hands. The premises were raided, the occupants rounded up and the building destroyed as we watched from a safe distance. I was horrified and realised I was on my own now, so how could I risk losing him, as he was now my only friend.

I have also been told, directly by spirit, that in three previous lives I have been buried alive when in fact I was either deeply asleep or in a coma. I had also been buried alive under a fall of rock - all as a man, never as a woman. This may account for the fact that in my mid-50s I had difficulty staying asleep for longer than an hour or two at a time.

A darker memory was to do with a lady I worked with who became my superior. Following a serious mistake in her first week as boss, which was someone else's fault not mine, but for which she blamed me, she took a dislike to me. This affected my work in that she lost no opportunity to send me elsewhere, usually to the basement to do filing. I had no ill feelings towards her and neither I nor her colleagues could understand the vehemence of her dislike of me – one colleague said she "was paranoid about Helen".

It appeared that in a past life, a long time ago, she was a prisoner who worked at a quarry along with many others. To get to and from the quarry the prisoners were strung together by chains linking their headbands of metal. At the site these circular headbands were used for discipline by pulling down on the chain hanging at the back for instant effect or by tightening the screws to pull the two halves of the band of metal tighter for a more permanent effect. On the inside of the metal at each of the temples was a patch of metal burrs to induce pain. And, guess what, I was the one in charge of the workforce!

It seems that she was looking forward to the fast-approaching time when she could go home, and was getting a bit high-spirited, so I had ordered her screw to be tightened. This had never before been necessary for her. [We were both male in that life, but I will stick to the feminine terms]. Unbeknown to me she had a thin skull and this had fractured it, causing her death. No wonder she disliked me so much!

It might also explain why in this life I have been subjected to the terrible pain of migraines, now, thankfully, lessened.

Much later I learnt that this was in the 12th century and was 'Germanic'. I also identified three more people who had been prisoners under my control, who still suffered head pains, and of whom I sought and obtained forgiveness. Two of these I had helped considerably in this life with my skills as healer and spiritual counsellor. The other had become my mentor, and it was through her that I was made aware of the above.

This also illustrates how very unwise it is to seek knowledge of past lives unless you are very sure that you can cope with whatever surfaces, for many lives will have been horrible. To be born with no memory of our past is a blessing, as one can start with a clean sheet. If there is any chance that you would be unable to cope with any feelings of vengeance, anger, grief, shame or anything else negative, then it is better not to know.

It is also better not to know if it might induce in you feelings of pride, arrogance or superiority.

Although it may be a good idea to ask the angels to help you forgive anyone who has hurt you - and to ask forgiveness from anyone you have hurt - in any lifetime. This will have to come from your heart, of course, or it will not work. You do not have to remember them for this to work, but you must be sincere.

It may also be a good idea to ask the angels to help you cut cords and rescind all vows that you have made in past lives that are no longer for your highest good. We have all made vows of poverty, chastity, loyalty – including marriage vows – silence etc. Angels are appointed to help you keep these vows so they must be released from their tasks. I have found 'The Karma Release Meditation' cd by Diana Cooper to be very helpful, and highly recommend it.

PART THREE

Miscellany

"All the world's a stage, and all the men and women merely players: they have their exits and their entrances; and one man in his time plays many parts…"

William Shakespeare
"As You Like It"

Your Higher Self

Firstly you need to realise that you are not your body. Your body is a garment you wear in order to exist on this Earth.

Through your body you can experience all your soul wishes to and needs to this time around. For this reason you have the physical conditions you need, including the personality.

The part of you that incarnates is only a tiny part of your total self. Picture a multi-faceted diamond. These facets are like the many aspects of your soul and in any one incarnation only a few are needed. The rest is still connected and can be accessed by you at any time. We call this part of you your Higher Self, as opposed to the Lower Self that operates in this material world. The Higher Self contains the distillation of your many incarnations, and so can be drawn on for inspiration and guidance. This is where many people's 'hunches', 'gut feelings' and intuition comes from.

I know someone born the son of a slaughterman who was taken as young as four years old into an abattoir. He went on to become a slaughterman himself, a trade he practised for many years. In later life he became a healer and was able to offer healing, along with spiritual wisdom, to this community – a closed community who needed one of their own to open their minds to these new ideas.

He was a kind, generous and gentle soul. I asked him how he could have worked in such an atmosphere of death and suffering. He replied that he also had wondered this, and one day he 'saw' himself amongst a large group of souls, all waiting to incarnate. They were told that there was this special group of people who needed someone to go in and help them progress. It would not be easy. It would need an insider to take the Light to them, someone who knew their ways and was one of them – a trusted member of their community. My friend put his hand up and volunteered. As a result he was given all that he needed for the task, including the right personality to be able to handle it.

This may have been a memory from his Higher Self, as indeed many of my memories of my past lives may have been. Also much guidance can come from your accumulated wisdom; it does not have to come from spirit helpers, angels or indeed from priests or other holy people. You are spirit here and now – just in a physical body. You do, however, need to learn to be still and listen to that 'still small voice within'.

We are told from many sources that this world of ours is all illusion, created by us, individually and collectively. Picture this as a giant, complex computer game, which we have each opted to play. We choose our side, our character and our tasks but we get so immersed in the game we forget that it **is** a game. We forget we are only playing, and can choose to take the game in another direction or we can opt out whenever we want. We can have a rest then perhaps choose to come back as a different character, at a different level, and with different tasks – or we may choose to try the same game again, in order to improve our performance. The idea is to get better at it with time and practice, so that we can progress up many levels, and when we have done all that we want to with this game, we can leave it and move on to something else.

It is important to not get so enmeshed in the game that it gets you down. If you find yourself taking it all too seriously then you need to remind yourself it is only a game that you have chosen to play, and can opt out of at any time. The game is meant to teach, but also to be enjoyed. If you are not enjoying it, then change your mind and view it differently or change the game to one you do enjoy.

Never forget that you are so much more than you know, with huge potential. However bad your situation may seem it can be hugely improved by changing the way you think of it. I'm sure you can think of two people in similarly bad situations where one person is utterly crushed by it and the other puts on a brave face and carries on quite cheerfully, even perhaps helping others.

To begin to realise your potential you will need to be mindful of it, and to encourage it at every opportunity. Do not allow negative thoughts to weigh you down. When any occur to you try to change them to a positive thought. Remember that the Universe wants you to have your heart's desire, and will bring to you those things that you focus on. So do not focus on the negative, but replace all such thoughts with the positive outcomes you desire.

It will help enormously if you set aside time every day for contemplation, reflection and/or prayer and meditation. This will enable you to get in touch, and stay in touch, with your Higher Self.

The ideal is to make your whole life a meditation – i.e. to always be mindful. Until then do not think that you have to sit in silence to meditate, doing nothing else. I used to meditate whilst washing-up or ironing, for which you only need half a brain. Put on some gentle music, ask your guide or the angels to draw close, and just set your mind free. Do NOT do this whilst driving or operating machinery.

Remember that prayer is asking - meditation is listening.

Energies and Dimensions

The whole of life is energy – constantly changing its form and shape, and in constant contact with the whole. Your body is held together by energy, and is animated by the energy that is the true you, without which your body would return to the earth from whence it came.

It would be arrogant and stupid of us to assume that all we can see, hear, touch, smell and taste is all there is. We know there is more. We know, for instance, dogs can hear sounds well out of our range of hearing, as can bats. Various animals have far greater powers in certain areas than we do – we do not dispute this. They are not just physical powers, but are often powers to connect to something beyond our scientific understanding - birds migrating thousands of miles, and still returning to where they were born; eels travelling across oceans to a place they have never been, and later finding their way back to their birth-place; huge flocks of birds swirling around in the air, yet never crashing into each other. Nature is indeed wonderful, and still in many ways mysterious.

Imagine I am talking to you on a lonely grassy hillside and tell you that you are surrounded by many sounds you cannot hear, and sights you cannot see. I could easily prove it to you.

All I need to do is suggest installing banks of televisions and radios. If they were all tuned into different channels and stations there would be an overwhelming cacophony of sounds and so many different pictures that you would have to close your eyes to escape them. Add to this many people on their laptops and mobile phones and you will realise just how many different frequencies would be involved. You would suffer severe sensory overload.

These sights and sounds didn't come with the machines – they were already there. They came via the machines, each of them using a different frequency. Also, think of x-ray machines, night-vision cameras, and infra-red sensors and you may begin to see the huge scope for things outside of our normal five senses.

There are many more frequencies than we have machines to harness them, and it is these frequencies that healers, mediums and clairvoyants use. It is from these frequencies that we are able to receive messages from our loved ones in 'the beyond', and to occasionally get peeks into other realms, e.g. ghosts or fairies, who exist in other dimensions.

Maybe one day there will be machines for this – experiments have been made to capture healing frequencies via machines, and also voices from beyond, with limited success as yet.

As we go through life we leave an imprint of our energies on places and objects, of varying degrees of strength according to the amount of our use and the strength of our feelings. These can be accessed by those open to those frequencies as in psychometry. They can also appear as the whole person and situation, as in ghosts - which are simply 'recordings' that can be accessed on occasions by deliberately or accidentally tuning in to the relative frequency, but cannot be altered, except by being erased. Unlike spirits these ghosts cannot be communicated with, in the same way that actors in a film cannot be communicated with. Many hauntings come into this category – just think of all those headless horsemen who ride at the full moon on a windy night, or the nuns who walk the same paths and enter doors that have long since gone. These kind of repetitive occurrences are ghosts. Any hauntings where different things occur require an intelligence to make them happen and are therefore spirits.

Science operates mainly on the basis of being able to reproduce things in the laboratory, and thus scientists often find it hard to accept anecdotes regarding the paranormal, seeking other explanations. That's fine. That's how science progresses. Some of the spiritual healing can be verified by medical tests, but are often put down to unexplained factors, partly because many people do not tell the medical professionals that they have been having healing.

I would say, though, that it is like trying to prove that love exists to someone who has never experienced it. How do you? Love cannot be reproduced in a laboratory, or under controlled conditions. If you seek it, it can be elusive. If you don't, it can appear out of nowhere. Many paranormal experiences are very similar in that respect.

When we 'die' our spirit leaves our body and continues operating in a different dimension – i.e. at a different frequency, and in another body operating at that frequency.

There are many different frequencies available, and the spirit gravitates, or is guided, to the one that it is most comfortable in. There it will discover all that it needs to continue on its path.

Those who have lived spiritually-motivated lives will gravitate to a higher frequency than those who have lived very material lives. It does not depend on how religious you have been, but on how spiritual, which is an entirely different thing. Many religious people are also spiritual, but many are not. Deathbed confessions are of little value beyond the basic recognition of wrongdoing. On the other hand many non-religious people are spiritual, and spend much time helping others.

So when people seek contact with 'the dead' there are many different dimensions available. Those who seek to help 'stuck' souls will tune into what is called the astral planes, which are very similar to our own world. Those who seek to rescue souls will deliberately attune themselves to the lower astral planes, a dark and dismal world, in order to assist those ready to progress. Those who seek to contact relatives and friends usually find them in the astral planes, although they may need to access a slightly higher dimension. These are not ghosts as described above, but spirit who can be communicated with, and interacted with, and may very well know what has been happening in our lives since they 'died'. Depending on how long they have been there, they may also have learned a great deal.

Those who seek to channel the highest wisdom have the hardest job. They need to raise their vibrations (i.e. frequency) to the highest level possible, which can take many years of dedicated effort, and requires constant spiritual mindfulness (as indeed any ambition needs dedicated mindfulness to achieve). At the same time those from the highest realms will lower their vibrations in order to meet them halfway.

This ability to tune in to differing frequencies is a very subtle art which can be easily disrupted, and needs to be treated with the greatest respect. Many people have a natural ability to access certain frequencies, but no control over it – this can be very distressing.

In my years giving talks on such matters to groups of Year 10s (14 and 15 year olds) I soon found at least one from each group of about 30 would approach either me or the teacher afterwards with their own tale, often prefaced with "I've never told anyone this before, but...". The comment that moved me the most was from a girl to her teacher, saying that I had allowed her to believe what she wanted to believe. Another memorable one was from a boy who later included in his essay the words 'my hero Ms Bevan'! Soon I began my talk by saying that I expected one or two of them will have already had a paranormal experience, and as I looked around the group I would see one, two or even three, nodding. On this basis I estimate that, at the very least, ten per cent of people have had paranormal experiences of their own, with more knowing someone close to them, that they have complete trust in, able to report at least one.

This raises the question in my mind – at what point does the paranormal become normal? The answer is obvious – when to enough people it becomes so normal that it is accepted by the greater proportion of society, even though many of them will not have had personal experience of it. In many societies it is and always has been the norm, and within my own spiritualist community - within the greater Western society - it is also considered quite normal, especially the healing side of it. It has become much more acceptable now than it was thirty years ago. This begs the question as to who defines what is normal? In our western civilisation, surely it is the media, but within each of our 'societies within society' it is us.

So it is up to every individual to make up their own minds, and I have no doubt that in my life, and in the lives of many thousands of people, it is accepted as normal, albeit still considered extraordinary, much as artists, musicians etc. are normal but sometimes extraordinarily gifted.

Opening Sacred Spaces

If you wish to meditate, do healing of any kind, or connect with spirit or your helpers from the realms of Light, you need firstly to make yourself a sacred space to protect yourself and others, and to make it easier for those from the higher realms to link with you.

If you wish only for contact with your deceased friends and relatives, you still need to protect yourself from any lower vibrational souls, otherwise you may get more than you bargained for.

Be aware that like attracts like, so make sure you are in a fit state for your purpose – you can't do this successfully if you are in a rush, or in any way emotional.

After preparing yourself, arrange the physical space that you have in a manner that suits your purposes – so maybe you set up an altar; light candles; burn incense or oils; set special music playing… The very act of this preparation helps to calm you and create the right mood, both in the room and in yourself.

Then you need to call upon your guide and helpers from whichever realms you need or want at that time, stating the purpose for which you want or need them. Please reach to the highest level that you can envisage, with no doubts but that you will be heard, and that your call will be responded to. You need to ask them to join with you, and to give you their protection; to make the vibrations of your space harmonious for your purposes; to bless you and your intended purpose…

A sample of the kind of words to use is:-

***Divine Spirit**, (or Dear Friends; Dear Lord; whatever you are happy with)*
I ask that you and your angels draw near and bless me (us) with your Presence. Please bring your Love, Power and Protection, and cleanse and sanctify this space for the purpose(s) of…
Please transmute any negative or inharmonious vibrations with the violet flame into Love and Light.
I ask that you and any others from the realms of Light who wish to work with me (us) at this time make your presence felt, and join with me (us) in Love.
When I am (we are) finished here, please again cleanse this space and make it harmonious for its normal purpose(s).
Any surplus energies please use for the benefit of…
I am (we are) very grateful for the help you give me (us).
Thank you.

Blessed be. Om Shanti. Amen   *(Or whatever you prefer).*

I include the last part in case you are interrupted and forget to close this sacred space, as sometimes happens, but ideally you will at the end say a simple prayer of gratitude and closure. Remember also that you need to close yourself down before you again engage with the everyday world, *[see next chapter]*.

You may also like to say the Lord's Prayer, thinking of every phrase, as over the centuries its use has built up a great power. If you have a suitable set prayer from any other religion then that also can be used.

It helps to have a regular time, as your spirit friends can then be ready and waiting to help you. Early morning is a good time if you can manage it, as it is so quiet and still, but if you can't then maybe midday when many people are sending out thoughts for the world - or a set time in the evening, this would help you to relax after the days' work, and so get a better sleep. If, like us, you do not keep regular hours then ask for help just prior to commencing.

You may wish to be used in your sleep to help mankind, or the Universe generally; or to gain knowledge and understanding. I would advise, though, that you also ask to awake refreshed, as often such work can leave you feeling tired the next day.

Our spirit friends don't always know the effect they have upon us, so please feel free to tell them that they are asking too much. Remember me saying I had to ban them from the bedroom? And when I had to ask them not to freeze my hand?

Never forget that it is <u>you</u> who needs to be in control of what is required.

White Eagle has what he calls the 'magic hours' – his symbol of the equal-arm cross in a circle is like an analogue clock-face. So his 'magic hours' are 12, 3, 6 and 9, which are the points of the cross. At these hours his followers are asked to link in with him and the spirit healers to bring healing to oneself, others and/or the world. There are other groups that link in at noon, and others that link for healing at 10, both a.m. and p.m. This is local time, and means that there is a wave of Light being sent around the world all day long.

When people say "why doesn't God do something about it?" they must realise that <u>we</u> are the agents God uses. This is a planet of free-will, and that free-will is mostly exercised within our own thoughts. Our situation in life was chosen by us before we were born in order to facilitate our spiritual progress. Our reactions to those situations that we find ourselves in is how we show what progress we have made, or not, as the case might be. So getting into the habit of marking the 'magic hours', and meditating daily, keeps us spiritually mindful, and so helps us to progress, thus easing many of life's problems. You feed your physical body several times a day. You need to do the same for your spiritual body.

I found a useful practice, when I was walking to work, or waiting for a bus, was to mentally do the following chakra balancing exercise. Send your thoughts to beneath your feet and link in with the earth, thus grounding yourself, then mentally draw up the energies of the earth through the back of all your main chakras to the crown. Then link in with the highest sphere you can drawing down those energies through the front of all your chakras to the earth. As you breathe in draw them up, and as you breathe out bring them down. As you circulate them in this way you will bring your chakras into balance, and clear any that may be blocked. You may actually feel one or more blocked, and will find that a bit of extra effort will unblock it. You will also find yourself to be physically and spiritually balanced and energised. Try it for yourself.

Closing Down

When you have opened your chakras doing spiritual work - which often happens naturally as your compassion flows to people, animals and situations – it is wise to close them again so that you can safely work in the normal world again. If your love is not flowing outwards you can act as a sponge instead, absorbing the feelings around you, which are often negative in nature, and which may leave you feeling unaccountably depressed, in pain, or tearful.

I use the following method of closing down:-

Work your way down the seven chakras from the top.

Picture each chakra as an open flower. You may like to picture the flowers in the colours of each chakra, but don't worry if you can't: –

- crown – violet
- third eye (centre of forehead) – purple or dark blue
- throat –blue
- heart – green
- solar plexus – yellow
- sacral (two inches below the navel) - orange
- root chakra (the base of the spine) - red.

Picture each one in turn closing for the night, and withdrawing into the chakra.
(Alternatively you could picture the hatch of a submarine slamming shut, or window shutters closing. Whatever works for you. It is the intention that matters most).

If you have difficulty visualising, as many people do, then simply instruct the chakras as above and know that this will happen.

Seal each closed chakra with a sacred symbol. Having learnt this sequence from my local White Eagle group, I use the White Eagle symbol of an equal-arm cross of light within a circle of light, but you may prefer the Christian cross, a rose, a pyramid, a star, an oak tree…

Using deep breaths, draw light on the inward breath from below the left foot up the left side of the body to the crown, and drop it on the outward breath down the right side of the body to below the right foot. Do this seven times.

Now, on the inward breath draw light up from below the feet to above the crown in a seven-fold spiral, clockwise around the body, and on the outward breath drop it straight down to below the feet.

You are now closed and sealed.

You need to do this after every time you open up – and remember that you may not have been aware of opening up, as it often happens unconsciously. It is a good idea to do it prior to leaving your home, (hopefully you have made your whole home a safe, protected sacred space). I used to do it on my five minute walk to work, after first having done the chakra balancing exercise that I explained in the last chapter.

For extra protection you could imagine yourself in your egg-shaped aura, however big you think it is, surrounded by a flexible membrane through which no vibrations lower than yours can enter. Fill it with a lovely colour of your own choice, which may vary from time to time, as your needs change.

For emergency protection you may picture a hooded cloak being quickly wrapped around you completely covering you from head to toe – I would suggest visualising blue, purple or gold. Alternatively you could picture a golden dome or pillar of light being dropped over you. You can also do this for someone else, your children for instance. It will not interfere with their freewill, as if their Higher Self does not wish it then it will not happen. (This is similar to the way distant healing works).

Also, if you feel you are being drained of vital energy put your left hand over your solar plexus, with your right hand on top – or just cross your arms, whilst mentally instructing that chakra to close.

If you are open then needy people can drain the energy from you, like water finding its own level. Many people experience this when visiting ill friends or family – when they leave they feel drained, but the one they have visited feels energised. An exchange of energies has taken place, and the one who benefits just loves such visits, although they usually have no idea that they are draining you.

You can still help them, without draining yourself, by asking for the energy to be channelled, so that it goes <u>through</u> you not <u>from</u> you.

Poems

I wrote this when my world revolved around two pre-school children.

Going under

O so weary, all alone,
Where has all the gladness flown?
Does my loved one understand?
Will he, can he, lend a hand?

Sinking down in deep depression,
Depths that Time alone can lessen.
No-one near with whom to share
Black, black moods of dark despair.

Youthful freedom now forgotten,
Joys of motherhood turning rotten.
In the grip of darkest gloom,
Can I overcome it soon?

Staring at the same old things,
My mind going round in rings.
Imprisoned by these duties heavy
Responsibility takes its levy.

Weeping tears of sheer frustration;
Wife and mother now my station.
Dreams of being a healer/medium
Buried under days of tedium.

O so weary, all alone,
Have I years of gladness sown?
Will my loved ones understand,
Should I not gain the upper hand?

As you can see I did get through that phase! And achieve my dream!

Panoramic view of the twin hills with Caer Caradoc on the right.

This poem and photo are included courtesy of our friend Dave Pearse who took the photo of Keith in the country lane below Caer Caradoc, Shropshire, with a disposable camera, and later wrote the poem, (before the film was developed). He had seen nothing unusual, and no other photos on the film showed anything unusual.

We were on Vegan Camp at Cardington, Shropshire, at the time, from where I took the panoramic photos. Prior to our visit to Caer Caradoc (Caer is Welsh for hill), which locally was regarded as the hill where Caradoc made his last stand, he had persuaded us to link in with the site. We had become aware of warriors from those days still fighting on Caer Caradoc and had, of course, helped clear any that were still stuck. (The fighting itself may have been just residual energy).

It appears to us to be a warrior with a sword and shield, standing tall and proud.

CAER CARADOC

Rising tall, proud and grand,
High above Shropshire's green sweet land,
A hill cloaked deeply in history,
And shrouded in exciting mystery,
Where in quiet moments may be heard,
And seen a ghostly vision blurred,
Of brave devoted warriors of long ago,
Who held to the last against the invading foe,
Till slaughtered at their goddess' breast,
On that sacred hill their bodies rest,
Brave Caradoc and his tribesmen bold,
Never freedom, land or goddess sold,
Rather than cower like timid mice,
Chose instead the ultimate sacrifice,
So great was Caradoc's will to fight,
That only when totally battered by Roman might,
Was he seized and taken slave,
But even the Romans were awed by a chieftain so brave,
And so out of honour and respect,
Set him free from their net.
But evermore Caradoc Hill stands above the land.
As silent witness to the Briton's last stand.

© *DAVE PEARSE 2005*

Gratitude

There is a veil of doubt and fear
That hides from sight what <u>might</u> appear.
It causes us to shrink away
Instead of greeting each new day
With uplifting thoughts of hope
That will enable us to cope
By showing us the many things
Of love and beauty each day brings.

Enjoy the beauty of the sun,
The way each season has its run.
Marvel at the everyday
Miracles that come your way –
Flowers, showers, birds and bees,
Rainbows, clouds, scents that please…

Remember, too, that things unseen
That touch your life have always been –
A mother's love, an angel's kiss,
Many things you'd sorely miss.
The healing touch of someone dear
Helping you through your year.
There is indeed much to bless,
So open your heart to happiness!

Helen Bevan 2008

Affirmations

And finally, some affirmations that I have devised and found to be helpful. Ideally you should devise your own, so feel free to adapt these if you so wish. Saying them frequently will re-programme your brain, thus helping you to become more positive and focussed on your desires, not your problems, and thus help the Universe to manifest them.

I am a part of God and so am divinely guided.

I am helped by, and grateful to, spirit guides and helpers from the realms of Light, and by workers for the Light from other dimensions.

It is my intention that I be secure, happy and successful.

It is my intention that I receive love and give love in all things that I do.

It is my intention to be healthy and full of vitality throughout my waking life.

It is my intention to sleep soundly every night and wake refreshed every morning.

It is my intention that I be provided for in abundance according to my needs.

It is my intention to overcome the limitations so far put upon me and to comfortably grow into my full potential.

May all things that I ask be always for my highest good, and the highest good of all.

I hope you have enjoyed this book and that it has perhaps given you more confidence in your own experiences, and maybe it has helped you to keep on keeping on.

May the Universe smile upon you.

Helen currently leads a monthly meditation group in Brislington, Bristol.

Please contact her if you would be interested in attending.

She and Keith ran a weekly drop-in healing clinic in Fishponds, Bristol, every Thursday 2-6 p.m. – except in Aug – from 2006 - 2011.

> *Have you got ghostly problems?*
> *With things that go bump in the night?*
> *We'll have a go at clearing these,*
> *Try to put things right!*
> *If we don't clear it first time,*
> *We'll have another session*
> *But we can't guarantee*
> *To help with their progression.*
>
> *Keith Bevan*

Helen is available for healing and psychic clearance (with Keith); talks, Spiritualist services or clairvoyant evenings. They do not charge but do expect their expenses to be well covered.

Tel:- 0117 932 2411
    e-mail:- helenbevan@ymail.com
    www.hauntingsandhealings.co.uk